T0328196

Cambridge Elements ≡

Elements in Business Strategy
edited by
J.-C. Spender
Kozminski University

SUSTAINABLE VALUE CHAINS IN THE GLOBAL GARMENT INDUSTRY

Rachel Alexander
Copenhagen Business School & University of Johannesburg

Peter Lund-Thomsen
Copenhagen Business School

CAMBRIDGE
UNIVERSITY PRESS

Shaftesbury Road, Cambridge CB2 8EA, United Kingdom

One Liberty Plaza, 20th Floor, New York, NY 10006, USA

477 Williamstown Road, Port Melbourne, VIC 3207, Australia

314–321, 3rd Floor, Plot 3, Splendor Forum, Jasola District Centre, New Delhi – 110025, India

103 Penang Road, #05–06/07, Visioncrest Commercial, Singapore 238467

Cambridge University Press is part of Cambridge University Press & Assessment, a department of the University of Cambridge.

We share the University's mission to contribute to society through the pursuit of education, learning and research at the highest international levels of excellence.

www.cambridge.org
Information on this title: www.cambridge.org/9781009217712

DOI: 10.1017/9781009217729

First published 2023

A catalogue record for this publication is available from the British Library.

ISBN 978-1-009-21771-2 Paperback
ISSN 2515-0693 (online)
ISSN 2515-0685 (print)

Sustainable Value Chains in the Global Garment Industry

Elements in Business Strategy

DOI: 10.1017/9781009217729
First published online: May 2023

Rachel Alexander
Copenhagen Business School & University of Johannesburg

Peter Lund-Thomsen
Copenhagen Business School

Author for correspondence: Rachel Alexander, ral.msc@cbs.dk

Abstract: The widespread prevalence of economically, socially, and environmentally unsustainable practices in global value chains is a pressing international challenge. The way to improve systems and practices in the complex networks that characterise contemporary production processes is not clear-cut. Finding solutions requires innovation. This Element examines the structures of garment value chains and explores how innovation related to sustainability is taking place within these chains. Furthermore, it identifies barriers and opportunities for innovations to break through and stimulate industry-wide change.

Keywords: global value chains, sustainability, innovation, garments, corporate social responsibility

ISBNs: 9781009217712 (PB), 9781009217729 (OC)
ISSNs: 2515-0693 (online), 2515-0685 (print)

Contents

Preface

This Element focusses on sustainable value chain innovation. *Why write an Element on sustainable value chain innovation in the global garment industry?* We wrote this Element because we felt that there was a need for a concise and authoritative introduction to the subject of sustainable value chain innovation. The global garment industry is used as a case in point which can provide students, academics, and practitioners with a comprehensive overview of ongoing developments in this new and exciting, yet understudied, field of research, policy, and practice. As authors, in our work on sustainability we have both carefully studied and followed ongoing international developments in the global garment and textile industries. In short, we believe that the global garment and textile industries are now under pressure to reinvent themselves in ways that will ensure their long-term economic, social, and environmental stability and survival (Muthu & Gardetti, 2020). We see these pressures arising from multiple sources.

First, following the Paris Agreement on climate change, the need for limiting global warming has been reiterated in a dramatic fashion, requiring its signatories – almost 200 countries and the European Union (EU) – to work together towards limiting global warming (Jensen & Whitfield, 2022; United Nations, n.d.). Global garment and textile production creates significant contributions to greenhouse gas emissions. Yet there is still an evident knowledge gap in relation to how to significantly reduce the fashion industry's greenhouse gas emissions (Berg et al., 2020). Responding to this need, the United Nations' Fashion Industry Charter for Climate Action (FICCA) has been set up with a mission to drive the industry to net zero emissions by 2050. Through its various working groups, FICCA seeks to develop new insights into combatting CO_2 emissions in the industry by identifying and amplifying best practices, facilitating and strengthening collaboration among relevant stakeholders, joining resources, and sharing the tools and knowledge to enable the sector to achieve its climate targets (FICCA, 2021). Hence, there is now a large-scale interest in developing new solutions, or innovations, to facilitate a transition towards a climate-neutral garment industry (Kumar, 2017).

Another development has been the growth of new actors and alliances that have emerged with a view to facilitating the transition towards more sustainable garment value chains, such as the Ellen MacArthur Foundation, the Better Cotton Initiative, the Global Fashion Agenda, and the Sustainable Apparel Coalition (Ghori et al., 2022; Jensen & Whitfield, 2022). Such organisations also seek to facilitate new insights and new ways of working and organising in garment value chains and introduce new technological tools and solutions such as those that can help in increasing the transparency of industry practices (Muthu & Gardetti, 2020; Alexander & Lund-Thomsen, 2021). These organisations and initiatives seek to facilitate broader sustainability transitions within the industry in ways that go beyond individual brand/retailer and supplier initiatives. Instead they seek to introduce broader systemic changes in the industry, in particular through joint collaboration and efforts to find answers to sustainability challenges – for instance, making cotton production more socially and environmentally sustainable – in areas where existing technological and business-oriented solutions may not be immediately apparent (Riisgaard, Lund-Thomsen, & Coe, 2020).

In addition, it has become increasingly obvious in recent years that the dominant fast-fashion industry model, which has promoted overconsumption and waste in the industry, is incompatible with a broader sustainability transition (Peters, Li, & Lenzen, 2021). This model offers consumers the ability to buy large volumes of fashionable clothes at low prices and requires a highly responsive supply chain that can support a product assortment that is rapidly changing. It has contributed to high levels of pressure on production practices. For instance, increasing cotton production can intensify the use of polluting fertilisers and pesticides (Bick, Halsey, & Ekenga, 2018). Moreover, the constant pressure towards ever-cheaper prices and shorter lead times for suppliers has, in turn, placed a downwards price squeeze on suppliers (Anner, 2018), making it highly challenging for them to invest in environmental and social upgrading initiatives in their factories (Ponte, 2019). Furthermore, the model has also been associated with a wasteful 'use once and throw away' culture that has expanded the generation of post-consumption waste.

The drive towards sustainability innovation in global garment value chains must also be seen against the backdrop of increasing volatility and value chain disruptions that have taken place in the early twenty-first century (Lund-Thomsen, 2022). The global financial crisis of 2007/8 saw many suppliers across the Global South facing a global slowdown in demand (Palpacuer & Smith, 2021). In addition, the outbreak of the US-China trade war forced many companies to rethink their global garment sourcing patterns in order to deal with the impacts of the US sanctions against China (Lu, 2020).

Furthermore, the outbreak of Covid-19 led to massive, albeit temporary, disruptions to global garment value chains, with local suppliers and millions of workers in countries such as India and Bangladesh being particularly hard hit by the global economic slowdown (Anner, 2021). While many factories are now running at full speed again in these countries and many workers have now regained their employment within the industry, the Covid-19 crisis prompted many lead firms to find new ways of monitoring the social and environmental performance of their value chains at a distance when international travel was rarely possible (Lund-Thomsen, 2022). Suppliers also had to overcome the challenges involved in finding new ways of organising factory-floor and accommodation settings arising from the pandemic, such as the need to wear face masks, enforce social distancing, and rapidly vaccinate workers (Ruwanpura, 2022).

As the Covid-19 crisis appears to be receding, value chain challenges are continuing. Notably, the worldwide supply crises that emerged in late 2021 (Masters, 2022) have increased inflationary pressures (Rushe et al., 2022), and another round of value chain disruptions as a result of Russia's invasion of Ukraine (Simchi-Levi & Haren, 2022) has also forced companies in the global garment and textile industries to find innovative ways of overcoming structural challenges. Dealing with crises almost appears to have become a permanent feature of the world economy in recent years.

In addition to the increased worldwide pressures resulting from value chain disruptions, a range of new sustainability-focussed policy initiatives have emerged. Notably, a number of initiatives have been developed recently by the EU which have increased the international focus on the need for sustainable value chain innovation in the global garment and textile industries (Lund-Thomsen, 2022). First, in 2020, the EU introduced its new Circular Economy Action Plan, which was one of the main building blocks of the European Green Deal, Europe's new agenda for sustainable growth (EU, 2020). Second, in February 2022, the EU published its draft Directive on Corporate Sustainability Due Diligence, which sets out mandatory human rights and environmental due diligence obligations for corporations, along with civil liability regimes that enforce compliance and obligations to prevent, mitigate, or bring adverse impacts to an end (EU, 2022a). Third, two months later, in April 2022, this was followed by a Communication from the EU about the new EU Strategy for Sustainable and Circular Textiles (EU, 2022b).

While all these developments can be seen as drivers for change, the changes that are needed are yet to be defined. For example, many brands, retailers, suppliers, and sub-suppliers have limited expertise in the area of circular garment and textile production. Consequently, given the economic, social, and environmental challenges being faced, along with the pressures for change, the need for innovating new products, processes, and ways of orchestrating global garment value chains has never been more pertinent.

1 Introduction: Garment Value Chains and Sustainability

The garment and textile industries have been associated with diverse sustainability challenges. For example, they have been estimated to account for around 10 per cent of global CO_2 emissions, they consume huge amounts of water, and they involve jobs with poor working conditions (Locke, 2013; D'Ambrogio, 2014; Berg et al., 2020). While the widespread fast-fashion model reinforces these challenges, more sustainable systems are possible. Innovation is needed to create new systems. Potential solutions may lie in slow fashion (durable products produced on demand), circular economy models 'a model of production and consumption, which involves sharing, leasing, reusing, repairing, refurbishing and recycling existing materials and products as long as possible' (European Parliament, 2021) – and the creation of social enterprises, that is, businesses with social or environmental missions (EU, n.d.; Doherty et al., 2020). The emergence of new systems would impact the environment, workers, and economic development.

A key barrier inhibiting simple changes from transforming the global garment industry is that its production processes operate through global value chains (GVCs). Global garment value chains tend to involve complex networks that embody diverse sets of sustainability challenges (Alexander, 2022). Such networks often incorporate thousands of geographically dispersed producers contributing to production practices from disparate global locations, each making local level decisions. These networks are often highly fragmented and incorporate informal sector actors. Furthermore, this structure makes credible facts and numbers about global garment value chains difficult to ascertain (see Sturgeon, 2019).

According to the Organisation for Economic Co-operation and Development (OECD, 2018), the industry is characterised by several interrelated risks. These involve human rights and labour risks, which include child labour, discrimination, forced labour, occupational health and safety failings, violations of the rights of workers to establish or join a trade union and to bargain collectively, non-compliance with minimum wage laws, and wages that do not meet the basic needs of workers and their families. They also involve environmental risks which are related to hazardous chemicals, water consumption, water pollution, and greenhouse gas emissions. Finally, they involve integrity risks, which include bribery and corruption.

Sustainability innovation processes may play a critical role in dealing with the multiple, overlapping sustainability risks facing the global garment industry. Innovations can take place at micro or macro scales. With current systems creating a wide variety of sustainability challenges, there is a need for innovation within governance systems, production systems, or both.

Innovation can be seen as an outcome defined as 'a new or improved product or process (or combination thereof) that differs significantly from [a unit's own or other units'] previous products or processes and that has been made available to potential users (product) or brought into use by the unit (process)' (OECD & Eurostat, 2018). Innovation can also be seen as an action. It can be stimulated by a variety of triggers, which can be based on changing circumstances. The process of innovation can be seen to be driven through learning experiences which involve ongoing interactions between different actors, such as users and producers (Lundvall, 2016). Learning and innovation processes often emerge from routine activities but can also be the outcome of concerted research and development (R&D) activities. Thus, innovation can be carried out by diverse actors across the garment value chain.

To contextualise innovation for sustainability in the garment industry, it is important to understand how the industry currently works. While much diversity exists, some common steps in garment production can be identified. The first step often involves creating or collecting natural or synthetic fibres and yarns. Yarns are then turned into fabric. Finally, fabric is cut into pieces and sewn into garments (see Box 1 for more details).

Box 1 OVERVIEW OF TYPICAL ACTIVITIES IN GARMENT PRODUCTION VALUE CHAINS

Fibre production takes place in a variety of ways. These include farming (e.g., cotton or flax), animal rearing (e.g., wool or fur), and chemical synthesis (e.g., polyester made from petroleum or rayon made from cellulose in wood). Different types of technology and production techniques are used in each of these methods. Thread can be manufactured by spinning shorter fibres or produced by extruding a single long synthetic filament. These threads can be used to knit or weave fabrics. Diverse sustainability challenges accompany the manufacturing of thread and textiles. For instance, wet processing involves bleaching, dyeing, or applying treatments that impact the materials' appearance or function, during which vast amounts of chemicals, water, and energy are used (Berg et al., 2020).

Finally, garment production takes place in thousands of factories around the world, often involving several layers of subcontractors that carry out different parts of the assembly process. Garment production is often highly labour-intensive and associated with labour rights challenges such as a lack of formal contracts, payment violations, sexual discrimination and harassment, and a lack of social insurance (Locke, 2013). Garment manufacturing also encompasses other non-textile components, buttons for instance. These components are produced within their own value chains that have their own associated sustainability challenges.

Businesses in garment value chains are diverse. At the base of the chain, fibre production involves businesses ranging from the agricultural (e.g., cotton farmers) to petrochemical (e.g., polyester producers) sectors. Furthermore, their organisational forms also greatly differ. For example, the largest garment manufacturers are multinational firms with thousands of employees (Raj-Reichert, 2019), whereas the smallest include home-based microenterprises operating in the informal sector. Acting as suppliers in GVCs, producers make both standard products and custom-made orders. Producers also engage in diverse sustainability initiatives. These can have multiple motivations and can be geared towards demands from global buyers or be driven by local priorities (Langford, Nadvi, & Braun-Munzinger, 2022).

Actors at all points in garment value chains are spread around the world. As garment production requires high levels of manual labour, activities are often concentrated where labour costs are lower. The top-ten garment-exporting countries are displayed in Table 1. The exports reported by EU countries may involve production in which only the final stages were conducted in each country. The production of textiles and fibres can require more diverse types of processes and are not necessarily carried out in the same countries where garments are made (see Table 2). It is also important to note that while Tables 1 and 2 provide one way to gain a picture of the industry, by looking at exports, this perspective does not capture the full picture as many products within value chains are sold domestically.

Table 1 Top garment exporters in 2020

Country	Export value 2020 (billions USD)
China	124.5
Bangladesh	35.2
Vietnam	27.0
Germany	23.1
Italy	20.8
Turkey	15.0
India	12.2
Spain	11.6
Netherlands	11.1
France	10.7

Source: UN Comtrade (2023)
Note: Data reported by exporting countries, except for Bangladesh, which did not have self-reported data. The figure for Bangladesh is based on other countries' reported imports.

Table 2 Top textile and fibre exporters in 2020

Country	Export value 2020 (billions USD)
China	58.5
USA	10.8
India	9.8
Italy	6.1
Republic of Korea	5.9
Turkey	5.6
Vietnam	5.5
Taiwan	4.8
Germany	4.1
Japan	3.6

Source: UN Comtrade (2023)
Note: The figures in this table include HS Codes 50 (silk), 51 (wool, fine or coarse animal hair; horsehair yarn and woven fabric), 52 (cotton), 53 (vegetable textile fibres; paper yarn and woven fabrics of paper yarn), 54 (man-made filaments; strip and the like of man-made textile materials), 55 (man-made staple fibres), and 60 (fabrics; knitted or crocheted). Data reported by exporting countries.

At the end of the manufacturing processes, garment producers can sell their products directly to the public or they can sell them to wholesale buyers, such as fashion brands. Acting as buyers without owning their own production facilities, retailers and brands often dominate global garment value chains (Gereffi, 1999). Some of these companies have billions of USD turnover every year (see Table 3). Not only do these firms play a significant economic role through retail sales in many consumer markets but the items that they have manufactured also supply second-hand clothing markets in many parts of the world, which can comprise significant proportions of some national clothing industries (Brooks, 2019).

Large brands and retailers have been considered as chain drivers involved in orchestrating production processes carried out by tiered networks of producers (Gereffi, 1999). These lead firms can be considered as playing multiple roles in providing governance for sustainability. One aspect is having the ultimate say in design decisions.[1] Clothing designs have a key role to play in influencing the sustainability of garment manufacturing and consumption since they directly influence the types of production processes that are

---

[1] They can create their own designs, outsource design activities to third parties, choose designs created by suppliers, or collaborate with their suppliers in the design process.

Table 3 Top-selling apparel retailers in 2020

Company	Headquarters	Global apparel retail sales 2020 (billions USD)
Inditex, Industria de Diseño Textil SA	Spain	18.4
Fast Retailing Co Ltd	Japan	18.2
H&M Hennes & Mauritz AB	Sweden	15.4
Nike Inc	USA	15.2
Adidas Group	Germany	14.1
The Gap Inc	USA	12.9
Hanesbrands Inc	USA	7.9
Levi Strauss & Co	USA	7.0
PVH Corp	USA	7.0
LVMH Moët Hennessy Louis Vuitton SA	France	6.0
C&A Mode AG	Belgium and Germany	5.7

Source: Euromonitor (2021)

required and can determine whether product recycling options are feasible. Other aspects of lead firms' roles include setting prices and timelines and choosing production locations. Such decisions can have positive or negative implications related to sustainability outcomes. In their role as lead firms, many brands and retailers are engaging in a wide range of sustainability-related innovations that are often intended to influence the behaviour of producers, as we will discuss more in the body of this Element.

It is also important to note that not all commercial buyers of garments are similar to the world's largest lead firms. Large brands have been developing in emerging countries, such as Hailan Home from China, which had USD 3 billion in revenue in 2021 (Zhang, 2022), and the Indian company Aditya Birla Fashion and Retail, which had USD 1.1 billion in revenue in the 2022 fiscal year (Statista, 2022). Furthermore, the industry also includes many micro, small, and medium-sized brands and retailers whose behaviour and characteristics are quite distinct from those of large brands and retailers. These smaller companies do not have the same market power to dictate production and sustainability requirements to their suppliers. Moreover, wholesale buyers of clothing from manufacturers are not necessarily retail sellers. Alternately, some organisations (e.g., private sector firms and government agencies) purchase wholesale orders, such as employee uniforms, from producers.

Based in a range of global locations, businesses in garment value chains operate in diverse environments that involve different institutional pressures, including norms and rules (Scott, 2013). Furthermore, they experience distinct sustainability challenges and have divergent perspectives on sustainability (Alexander, 2018; Krauss & Krishnan, 2022; Lund-Thomsen, 2022). Across value chains, challenges can range from creating high levels of carbon emissions to using forced labour. In many cases, the technologies used in different parts of the world for the same activities can vary dramatically. For example, in some regions hand picking cotton is the norm and in others producers use high-tech harvesting equipment (Riisgaard et al., 2020).

Research into GVCs can provide unique insights into ongoing sustainability-related innovation processes by focussing on the reconfiguration of production and its developmental consequences. With a strong focus on value chain structures, we set out to answer five interrelated questions in this Element:

(1) What is sustainable value chain innovation?
(2) What are the key drivers behind this kind of innovation?
(3) Who are the actors involved in sustainable value chain innovation?
(4) Which innovative practices do these actors claim to engage in?
(5) Why are these practices likely to be (un)successful in achieving their aims?

The rest of this section introduces key concepts and outlines the contributions we intend to make before providing an outline of the rest of the Element.

1.1 Sustainability

The concept of sustainability is highly contested, while definitions of sustainability abound (see Box 2). In this Element, we consider sustainability to include economic, social, and environmental dimensions. From a business perspective, sustainability not only relates to companies maintaining financially viable operations; it also considers the ability of businesses to operate harmoniously within society, such as by providing employment and decent work and not causing social challenges. Additionally, it involves minimising the negative environmental impacts of business operations or, potentially, businesses generating positive environmental impacts. Sustainability in garment value chains is connected to diverse practices, which range from raw material production or extraction to manufacturing activities and waste disposal to transportation systems.

Box 2 Defining sustainability for businesses in global value chains (GVCs)
A hotly debated topic is whether corporate sustainability is different from corporate social responsibility (CSR) (Montiel, 2008). While both corporate sustainability and CSR are defined in multiple ways, a frequently used definition of CSR states that 'the social responsibility of business encompasses the economic, legal, ethical, and discretionary expectations that society has of organizations at a given point in time' (Caroll, 1979, p. 500). Corporate social responsibility has sometimes focussed on the social impacts of business operations while, at other times, it has, somewhat confusingly, been employed to describe the environmental aspects of business operations. Regarding corporate sustainability, this term often denotes whether current actions can exist 'without compromising the ability of future generations to meet their own needs' (World Commission on Economic Development, 1987, chap. 2, para. 1). Hence, some researchers and practitioners who refer to 'sustainability' emphasise that sustainable development should consider economic, social, and environmental pillars of business activities. Yet other researchers and commentators, sometimes implicitly, refer to sustainability as only including a narrower environmental lens, de facto referring to 'ecological sustainability'. Reflecting some of these variations in definitions, some brands, retailers, and suppliers in the global garment industry have established separate departments that are responsible for economic, social, and environmental risk management, whereas they are more integrated within the same business units in other companies. In this Element, we use the term 'sustainability'. We believe that it is more in line with recent debates about the future of the global garment and textile industries, including a green transition/climate change mitigation and adaptation, as well as human development.

The United Nations' Sustainable Development Goals (SDGs) are an international agreement that outlines global objectives related to having more sustainable global systems by 2030 (United Nations, 2015). The seventeen goals are outlined in Table 4. Whereas sustainable consumption and production are the explicit focus in SDG 12, activities in garment value chains can be linked to multiple goals such as poverty reduction (SDG 1), decent work (SDG 8), and climate change (SDG 13). At the same time, it is important to acknowledge that these are politically determined goals and that there may be inherent trade-offs within and across some of these goals. For instance, it may be difficult to secure

Table 4 The Sustainable Development Goals (SDGs)

Goal	Description
(1) No poverty	End poverty in all its forms everywhere.
(2) Zero hunger	End hunger, achieve food security and improved nutrition, and promote sustainable agriculture.
(3) Good health and well-being	Ensure healthy lives and promote well-being for all at all ages.
(4) Quality education	Ensure inclusive and equitable quality education and promote lifelong learning opportunities for all.
(5) Gender equality	Achieve gender equality and empower all women and girls.
(6) Clean water and sanitation	Ensure availability and sustainable management of water and sanitation for all.
(7) Affordable and clean energy	Ensure access to affordable, reliable, sustainable, and modern energy for all.
(8) Decent work and economic growth	Promote sustained, inclusive, and sustainable economic growth, full and productive employment, and decent work for all.
(9) Industry, innovation and infrastructure	Build resilient infrastructure, promote inclusive and sustainable industrialisation, and foster innovation.
(10) Reduced inequalities	Reduce inequality within and among countries.
(11) Sustainable cities and communities	Make cities and human settlements inclusive, safe, resilient, and sustainable.
(12) Responsible consumption and production	Ensure sustainable consumption and production patterns.
(13) Climate action	Take urgent action to combat climate change and its impacts.

Table 4 (cont.)

Goal	Description
(14) Life below water	Conserve and sustainably use the oceans, seas, and marine resources for sustainable development.
(15) Life on land	Protect, restore, and promote sustainable use of terrestrial ecosystems, sustainably manage forests, combat desertification, and halt and reverse land degradation and halt biodiversity loss.
(16) Peace, justice, and strong institutions	Promote peaceful and inclusive societies for sustainable development, provide access to justice for all, and build effective, accountable, and inclusive institutions at all levels.
(17) Partnerships for the goals	Strengthen the means of implementation and revitalise the Global Partnership for Sustainable Development.

Source: United Nations (2015)

energy sources that are clean, affordable, and reliable in many countries in the Global South and North (SDG 7). At the same time, the promotion of economic growth may not always be climate-friendly and create decent work (SDGs 8 and 13).

Achieving positive outcomes across economic, social, and environmental dimensions of sustainability is not possible for all business models. Sustainability challenges can be considered to exist if problems or tensions are experienced in any of the three dimensions of sustainability, as identified by any stakeholders or observers. However, identifying the best way to address sustainability challenges is not a straightforward process (Alexander, 2018). The process can be difficult and contentious, especially as different groups can have divergent perspectives and priorities (Krauss 2017; Riisgaard et al., 2020; Krauss & Krishnan, 2022; Lund-Thomsen, 2022). This uncertainty creates a space and a need for innovation (Alexander & Lund-Thomsen, 2021).

This Element presents diverse innovations that a range of actors are developing in relation to sustainability within garment value chains. In our discussion, we do not take a position on whether any of the innovations covered will create a more sustainable outcome. We solely consider that the innovation is in some way connected to sustainability challenges and/or objectives in the SDGs.

1.2 Value Chains

In this Element, we refer to a 'value chain' as 'the full range of activities which are required to bring a product or service from conception, through the different phases of production (involving a combination of physical transformation and the input of various producer services), delivery to final consumers, and final disposal after use' (Kaplinsky & Morris, 2002, p. 4). While our focus is on garments, a product, there are in fact many services that contribute to producing garments (e.g., fabric dyeing or transportation) (see Kleibert 2016).

Analysis of GVCs enables academics, students, and practitioners to obtain a better understanding of the steps through which production processes take place. Value chain structures are the product of historical developments, sometimes over centuries. Key elements of these structures include relationships between countries and innovations related to production practices.

A pivotal development in the formation of modern-day value chains was the expansion of new production techniques during the Industrial Revolution. The shift from craft-based production to larger industrial processes dramatically increased manufacturing efficiency. However, this change also created high levels of environmental degradation and working conditions that were strenuous and sometimes hazardous. Legislation was introduced to regulate production practices, including working conditions, in early industrialising countries. Subsequently, in the second half of the twentieth century, many manufacturing processes relocated to less regulated locations as part of a trend towards global outsourcing, leading to the emergence of increasingly fragmented value chains whereby multiple companies were able to contribute to the creation of products in geographically dispersed locations (Gereffi, 1994; Ponte et al., 2019).

Contemporary value chains have become increasingly large and fragmented. Large networks can connect a wide variety of enterprises creating products and services across multiple places, from rural, informal sector, agricultural-based businesses to large bureaucratic multinationals. The networks involved are dynamic and constantly in flux and can exist for a short time or many years. Connections can be relatively localised or link diverse global regions. As such, the networks have been described as multi-scalar with international, national, and local levels (Coe & Yeung, 2015).

Value chain analysis includes exploring governance related to the contexts where value chain actors operate. The behaviour of value chain actors can be seen to be shaped by three types of embedded locations (Henderson et al., 2002; Hess, 2004). One is network, which is based on the actors' position within a set of relationships. Network pressures can involve the power relationships that exist between buyers and suppliers (vertical connections) as well as the ways that actors are constrained due to their network position. The second is territorial, which is determined by geographic location. From their territorial location, value chain actors have horizontal relationships, which can incorporate a diverse set of actors such as states, non-governmental organisations (NGOs), and trade unions. The third location is societal, which is based on belonging to a particular culture or ethnic group. Owners' membership in particular social groups can shape firms' behaviours in multiple ways. Governance related to each type of location can be explored through considering institutional pressures, such as laws and norms, which operate at multiple geographic scales (Scott, 2013). Such institutional pressures shape the ways businesses behave in relation to communities and the natural environment and shape the dynamics of the markets in which such behaviours take place (Fransen, 2013). All three locations shape sustainability outcomes (Neilson & Pritchard, 2010; Lund-Thomsen & Coe, 2015; Gereffi & Lee, 2016).

1.2.1 Power Relationships in Value Chains

Power is a key concept within value chain analysis. According to Lukes (2005), power is something which an actor has the capacity to use but which the actor may or may not choose to exercise. If an actor chooses to exercise its power, this power can be targeted through different channels, involving both formal and informal mechanisms. Value chain actors wield different types of power in value chains. According to Dallas, Ponte, and Sturgeon (2019), these can be understood as operating within the dimensions of dyadic versus collective and direct versus diffuse that generate four forms of exercising power. One is bargaining power, which involves direct dyadic relations. A second is institutional power, which involves collective actors directly setting rules and standards. A third is demonstrative power, which involves individual actors (e.g., firms) acting as role models for others. A fourth is constitutive power, in which collective actors perpetuate common norms and values.

Relative power between actors is an important issue to consider in relation to sustainability in value chains. As diverse actors – within both the value chain and the broader institutional environment – tend to have divergent perceptions on defining sustainable forms of production, conflicts can arise. These types of conflicts between the deviating priorities of value chain actors have been described as value chain struggles (see Neilson & Pritchard, 2009). In short, it is important to understand value chains as contested fields 'in which actors struggle over the construction of economic relationships, governance structures, institutional rules and norms, and discursive frames' (Levy, 2008, p. 944). Overall, power relations are neither unidirectional nor structurally determined and involve instances of 'cooperation and collaboration' and 'conflict and competition' (Coe, Dicken, & Hess, 2008, p. 288).

Consequently, sustainable value chain innovation cannot be divorced from existing and sometimes highly unequal power relations within value chains. From this point of view, sustainable value chain innovation may reinforce and/or undermine existing power relations. In fact, sustainable value chain innovation may be resisted by actors within or outside of the chain to the extent that such forms of innovation undermine their existing positions within these chains. In particular, in some cases, innovations may reduce the profits of particular chain actors or exclude them from chain participation altogether. In this way, the multiple dimensions of power and their application in value chains sometimes make sustainable value chain innovation a contested process through which both winners and losers emerge (Alexander & Lund-Thomsen, 2021). In this Element, we include examples of value chain actors that have access to different forms of power as part of their engagement in sustainable value chain innovation.

1.2.2 Chain Governance

The dynamics shaping the relationships between lead firms and suppliers have been the focus of a large body of academic research. Two perspectives have been used to analyse these relationships (Bair, 2008). On one hand, these issues can be considered as part of the power relationships which link countries. On the other hand, these dynamics can also be explored by looking at the relationships between individual companies. Each of these perspectives has produced rich and informative research which helps to contextualise the actions of actors engaging in sustainable value chain innovation.

Considering national-level connections, one stream of research explores distinctions between 'the centre' and 'the periphery' (Hopkins & Wallerstein, 1977). Such considerations question the roles played by different countries within global production systems. Historically, these have often involved some countries seeing high levels of per capita income accompanied by high levels of consumption, while other countries have been responsible for high levels of global production processes in contexts where many people can barely afford subsistence levels of consumption. However, some of these patterns have begun to change in recent years. Emerging nations are seeing the growth of middle classes with more spending power and the growth of businesses that are becoming large lead firms in GVCs. These dynamics are creating increasing levels of what has been described as South–South trade (Horner & Nadvi, 2018).

Considering firm-level connections, relationships between firms in value chains have been analysed and categorised from multiple perspectives (Gereffi, Humphrey, & Sturgeon, 2005; Alexander, 2022). Value chains have been understood as being driven by actors such as individual brands and manufacturers or in some cases by multiple actors (Gereffi, 1994; Ponte & Sturgeon, 2014). For light manufacturing, such as garments, buyers have often been seen to have high levels of control over their suppliers (Gereffi, 1999; Gereffi et al., 2005). Recent studies have identified more complex power relationships within garment value chains, which include first-tier suppliers acting as lead firms (Kwon et al., 2021), and examples of varying governance relationships occurring across different parts of production processes (Alexander, 2022).

Inter-firm governance relationships can be influenced by the context in which production takes place. For example, a key dynamic is the nature of the innovation system(s) in which a firm operates. These systems can be considered to be 'constituted by elements and relationships that interact in the production, diffusion and use of new and economically useful knowledge' (Lundvall, 2016, p. 86). Innovation systems are often seen as being determined at the national level but can also be specific to subnational regions or production clusters. Innovation systems have been found to play a role in shaping the types of governance relationships that develop in GVCs by shaping the capabilities of suppliers (Pietrobelli & Rabellotti, 2011).

Norms and conventions create another dynamic shaping buyer–seller relationships (Ponte & Gibbon, 2005; Ponte & Sturgeon, 2014). One key

Table 5 Orders of worth and quality conventions

Orders of worth/quality conventions	Measure of product quality
Market	Price
Industrial	Formal quality testing
Domestic	Trust, repetition, and history
Civic	Social, labour, environmental, and collective impact
Inspirational	Spirit, personality, or newness
Opinion	Opinion poll, social media coverage, or subjective judgement by expert

Source. Framework developed by Ponte and Sturgeon (2014), drawing from Boltanski and Thévenot (1991)

aspect of this issue is quality conventions, which shape how a product's quality is assessed. Six forms of quality conventions, each associated with different measures of quality, have been identified (see Table 5). These quality conventions can overlap or be combined and change at different points along a value chain, such as raw materials being judged differently than final products.

Another type of governance actor that has not been discussed thus far is the end consumer in their role as buyer. Often sustainability-related ventures rely on consumers choosing to consider sustainability issues when making purchasing decisions (Henninger et al., 2017). Two key challenges can be identified related to the power consumers have over practices in GVCs. One issue is related to consumers' ability to make evidence-based decisions related to sustainability in value chains. In the current system, consumers choose from the choices presented to them and may have feelings of control, yet companies often choose what the consumers see. For consumer-facing ventures, consumers typically see the story presented by the company, which may focus on positive impacts of an initiative or product and ignore problematic aspects. A related concern is that this system can rely on consumers' opinions about which sustainability challenges they want to support, which may not be aligned with the urgency or scope of the most pressing global sustainable challenges. While systematically assessing impacts of production practices is a complex and contested process (Steubing et al., 2016; Reinales, Zambrana Vásquez, & Sáez de Guinoa, 2020; Palacios-Mateo, van der Meer, & Seide, 2021), consumers' preferences are based on personal opinions and the limited information on production and disposal processes that is publicly available (O'Roure & Ringer, 2016; Stankevich, 2017).

A second key issue is that the power of individual consumers differs. One element of this issue is that the level of spending a consumer carries out or their 'purchasing power' shapes their ability to express their perspective. As such, this model creates a situation in which voice is based on consumers' wealth. Relatedly, products which are intended to address sustainability challenges can be more expensive or more difficult to access and therefore are out of reach for many consumers.

Furthermore, value chain actors receive governance pressures from diverse actors, beyond those involved in vertical buyer-seller relationships (Gereffi & Lee, 2016). Key governance actors include public agencies, industrial organisations (e.g., business associations), NGOs, and media outlets. Each governance actor creates pressures through diverse mechanisms with a different range of reach. The mechanisms they use to govern can vary from setting rules to shaping public discourse.

1.2.3 Value Chain Risks and Public Messaging

A key distinction between value chains is that products' sustainability risk portfolios differ. One way to analyse these is by sector. Other important factors are where production is taking place and the type of technology that is being used. Key risks can be identified as being connected to each phase of a product's life cycle and can differ based on how an item is created, how it is used, and what happens to it after its primary use phase. Garment value chains are connected to diverse risk portfolios, which can be related to the production of each component part of a final garment and the processes and services that are used across the production, use, and afterlife of the item (OECD, 2018).

Some products and sectors have been given more attention than others when it comes to commercial actions related to sustainability (Jackson & Apostolakou, 2010; Brown & Knudsen, 2015). Key issues that can shape these dynamics are whether a sector is public-facing and whether a sector has prominent brand names. As such, the garment industry has received high levels of public focus, which has often concentrated on working conditions in garment factories associated with large global brands (Klein, 2000; Bartley & Child, 2011).

Dynamics of different sectors and products can shape how marketing takes place related to sustainable value chain innovation. In some cases, activities take place behind the scenes and are not actively marketed to buyers. In cases where innovation is marketed externally, this can focus on business-to-business relationships and/or business-to-consumer relationships. For example, innovation

taking place related to pesticide use on cotton farms may not be publicly adver-
tised to buyers of cotton, such as cotton ginning mills, whereas the development
of an innovative new material made from recycled inputs may be marketed by
textile producers to garment producers and be indicated on a consumer-facing
label on a final product (Alexander & Lund-Thomsen, 2021).

1.3 Innovation

We consider two dimensions of innovation in this Element. One is 'industrial
innovation' taking place in relation to production, use, and disposal. The other is
related to how industrial practices are governed. Governance systems, involving
lead firms, government agencies, and others, can seek to change production practices
through engaging in 'governance innovation'. This form of innovation involves
actions intended to shape the behaviour of industry actors, such as developing new
governance mechanisms, which may promote industrial innovation.

1.3.1 Change Pathways: Incremental vs Radical Innovation

Innovation is often considered as being incremental or radical. Incremental
innovation involves changes to existing products or services which may be
small improvements, such as making a process more efficient. Radical innovation involves a change that marks a large break from previous systems, such as
inventing a new product that transforms an industry. Radical innovation is
connected to disruptive change.

Lundvall (2016) points out that incremental and radical innovation can be
distinguished across economic and technical dimensions. Within this distinction,
it can be understood that incremental technical innovation can have a large
economic impact, for example if it solves a bottleneck. On the other hand,
a radical technical innovation may have a small economic impact if it does not
find a market. In addition to economic and technical dimensions, radical innovation can strongly deviate from existing systems in relation to other dimensions,
such as social aspects, business models, or infrastructure (Geels, 2019).

While boundaries between incremental and radical can be fuzzy, most innovation is incremental. Considering the multilevel perspective (see Box 3), socio-
technical regimes and path dependency can be seen to create pressures for
stability which mainly allow incremental change that follows stable trajectories
(Geels, 2004). While in some cases regime actors can be actively resistant to
change, strong levels of inertia can also exist which must be overcome for
change to be able to occur (Smith, Stirling, & Berkhout, 2005).

Klitkou et al. (2015) highlight nine lock-in mechanisms which can reinforce
an existing socio-technical system and inhibit radical change. First, *learning*

Box 3 The multilevel perspective

Industrial innovation can be seen to take place within a socio-technical system. This type of system includes technical elements involved in the production, diffusion, and use of technology, which incorporate items, knowledge, capital, labour, and cultural meaning (Geels, 2004). Socio-technical systems can be seen to be supported by actors who play roles related to supply (e.g., firms, research institutes, universities, and policy makers) and demand (e.g., users, special-interest groups, and media) (Geels & Kemp, 2007).

Socio-technical systems can be understood through the multilevel perspective, which considers interactions between processes at the micro, meso, and macro scales (Geels, 2002, 2004, 2019; Geels & Kemp, 2007). The macro level involves the socio-technical landscape where production takes place. Landscapes change slowly over decades and are beyond the control of individual actors. They form the environment where actors operate, including factors such as the macro-economic environment, culture, infrastructure, and macro-political trends. Relatively predictable technological trajectories exist within socio-technical landscapes, such as increasing efficiency of common products.

The meso level involves socio-technical regimes, which involve the 'semi-coherent set of rules' (Geels, 2002, p. 1260) upheld by groups of actors (e.g., firms, users, and policy makers) in a process that creates relative stability. Regimes do not have precise boundaries. Within the larger socio-technical regime, multiple specialised regimes coexist, with groupings related to fields such as design, product use, or infrastructure. These groups of regimes interact and overlap to create socio-technical regimes which provide a form of meta-coordination. Geels (2004, p. 905) describes socio-technical regimes as the '"deep-structure" or grammar of [socio-technical] systems [that] are carried by the social groups'. A socio-technical regime can be seen as shaping the norms in a sector, including the types of products that are created and how they are used.

Finally, at the micro level, niches exist as relatively protected spaces where actors have more freedom to break the rules and generate radical innovation. For example, niches can take the form of publicly subsidised research groups or small projects within larger companies. Niches can involve social networks that support innovations, such as links to producers.

A lot of research using the multilevel perspective has considered innovation as emerging within niches, with the most successful innovations spreading through a process that is based on an evolutionary model (Nelson & Winter, 1982). However, newer work has expanded to consider other paths to change – for example, looking at broader origins of innovation, such as grassroots initiatives, or considering that change can be driven from the top down (Geels, 2019).

effects involve experience with an existing technology leading to increased productivity and lower costs. Second, *economies of scale* can involve cheaper production when fixed costs are spread over a larger level of production. Third, *economies of scope* involve benefits created by being able to produce a variety of products. Fourth, *network externalities* involve products which benefit from being able to connect to an existing network, such as a phone network. Fifth, *informational increasing returns* involve widely adopted technology receiving higher levels of attention. Sixth, *technological interrelatedness* means that a technology benefits from being related to complementary technology. Seventh, *collective action* involves the creation and reproduction of societal norms and regulations which support an existing system. Eighth, *institutional learning effects* involve the creation of institutional structures which support the current system. Ninth, *differentiation of power and institutions* involves asymmetric power relationships, allowing strong political actors to shape the behaviour of others, and complementary relationships developing between institutions, both in ways that support the current system.

Radical change can be seen to occur in different ways. One way is that radical innovations can emerge within niches, where actors are often shielded from regime pressures (Geels, 2002). For example, actors working in a niche may not need to conform to the needs of the current market. Radical change can also emerge from the compounded influence of many incremental innovations (Genus & Coles, 2008). Considering the progression of innovation and change, three types of change processes can be identified as reproduction, transformation, and transition (Geels & Kemp, 2007). 'Reproduction' is considered as the processes which take place within a relatively stable socio-technical system. Such a system is supported by a relatively stable socio-technical landscape and regime. While innovations may be emerging in niches, they lack the opportunity to breakthrough due to strong pressure for stability. However, within overall stable systems, incremental innovation following existing trajectories, which can be seen as adhering to predictable patterns, occurs.

'Transformation' involves a change in the direction of the existing trajectory. The process can be stimulated by changes at the landscape level, which create pressure on the socio-technical regime. Regime rules can shift related to factors including 'changes in technical problem agendas, visions, goals and guiding principles, relative costs and incentive structures, regulations and perceptions of opportunities' (Geels & Kemp, 2007, p. 445). These changes can involve pushback from the existing regime. The pushback may involve negotiations, power struggles, and shifting coalitions. Change may be instigated by outside actors or public policy but the resulting transformation does not fundamentally undermine the position of actors involved in maintaining regulation of the existing regime. Overall, transformation is enacted by regime-level actors.

Finally, the most dramatic form of change can be considered as a 'transition'. Transitions involve 'a discontinuous shift to a new trajectory and system' (Geels & Kemp, 2007, p. 441). The shift in transportation from horse-drawn carriages to automobiles is an example of a transition. The process involves the creation of a new socio-technical system, which may have new regime actors.

1.3.2 Innovation Policy and Governance

Policy actors can play important roles in managing how industrial innovations emerge and scale. Notably, state actors can provide governance related to facilitating change or state actors can be part of regimes that stifle innovation (Smith et al., 2005). When seeking to stimulate innovation, policy actors can seek to promote incremental change that does not challenge current regimes or encourage more radical transition. Considering policy related to promoting transition processes, policy makers cannot directly control the complicated series of processes involved in socio-technical transitions (Geels, 2019).

Overall, governments can support the spread of innovation in multiple ways. These include facilitating interactions between actors to support learning, foresight, information exchange, and network development; stimulating radical innovation through funding R&D and conducting real-world experiments and demonstrations; shaping market conditions; articulating a vision; orchestrating coalitions that involve diverse actors, which may include other levels or branches of government; collecting and sharing information; translating practical experiences into policies; and creating regulations and standards, tax incentives, cap-and-trade policies, tariffs, subsidies, low-interest loans, and grants (Rotmans, Kemp, & Van Asselt, 2001; Geels, 2019). Policy interventions can be purposive, with state-directed attempts to steer technological developments, or more modest and involve state actors supporting change that is already taking place (Genus & Coles, 2008). The consideration of combinations of diverse government interventions in a 'policy mix' is seen as an important way to view how policy stimulates innovation and transitions (Kern, Rogge, & Howlett, 2019).

1.3.3 Innovation in Global Value Chains

This Element is particularly focussed on innovation in GVCs. Key research on this topic, as discussed further in Section 1.5, has explored learning dynamics, supplier upgrading, and innovation systems (Pietrobelli & Rabellotti, 2011; Jurowetzki, Lema, & Lundvall, 2018; Pietrobelli & Staritz, 2018, Lema, Pietrobelli, & Rabellotti, 2019). However, overall, more research is needed on the diverse elements of innovation in GVCs.

For example, an important factor to consider is how production network structures shape the potential for innovation. One angle is that production occurring within GVCs may stifle innovation. Notably, GVCs have been found to function as complex adaptive systems (Choi, Dooley, & Rungtusanatham, 2001), which have a tendency to absorb shocks and maintain structural patterns. In contrast to the risk of network structures inhibiting innovation, global connections can also stimulate innovation. Combining knowledge from different sources, geographic scales, and diverse actors has been found to promote innovation and regional development. However, some research has shown institutional diversity can create barriers to such processes (Strambach, 2017). To help understand such questions, this Element provides an introduction to a range of contemporary value chain innovation dynamics.

1.4 Sustainable Value Chain Innovation

In this Element, we consider sustainable value chain innovation to include innovation in or surrounding value chains which is connected to sustainability challenges or objectives. This innovation may take the form of new ventures or occur within existing organisations. Furthermore, in addition to including industrial innovation, it also includes governance innovation. Considering garment value chains, sustainability innovation can be seen to have multiple drivers and involve diverse actors.

1.4.1 Drivers of Sustainable Value Chain Innovation

Around the world, value chain dynamics can differ greatly. However, a number of key drivers for sustainable value chain innovation can be identified. One key driver is the existence of sustainability challenges, notably these include the global climate crisis and the repercussions being felt from the expansion of the fast-fashion model. The existence of these challenges can be seen as being created through gaps in public regulation (Gereffi & Mayer, 2006) and sustainable value chain innovation can be seen to be filling these governance gaps. When sustainability challenges are ongoing and regulation, or a lack of enforcement of regulation, is allowing problematic practices to continue, individuals and groups can voluntarily take action to address the problems.

Additionally, government and other stakeholder pressures can also be a driver of sustainable value chain innovation (Schaltegger & Wagner, 2011). Sustainability-focussed governance initiatives can specifically be designed to encourage private sector innovation. This can include setting sustainability goals and leaving companies to be creative in figuring out how to meet them – for example, setting limits on pollution (Zero Discharge of Hazardous Chemicals Programme, 2016). Governments and NGOs can also engage in supportive actions, such as running incubators or providing financial incentives, which seek to help start-ups with sustainability-related agendas. Such an approach can be seen in the integration of Strategic Sustainable Development at Inova's business incubator in Sweden (Blankenship, Kulhavy, & Lagneryd, 2009).

Another driver for sustainable value chain innovation is market demand. Demand for products marketed to the public as having sustainable characteristics is growing. Companies can engage in sustainability-related innovation in order to try to appeal to this market (Riisgaard et al., 2020). However, another side of market demand is that it can create drivers which perpetuate sustainability challenges. For example, customers seeking to keep up with the latest trends can buy and dispose of new items rapidly, which is particularly a problem when production processes create negative impacts and items are designed without consideration of their after-use life (e.g., not being recyclable or biodegradable). The low-priced fast-fashion system is a key example of this dynamic (Tokatli & Kizilgün, 2009).

Finally, a further driver and potential enabler can be found in the experiences of multiple crises which have repeatedly rocked the world and created changes to value chain structures and flows since the financial crisis which hit in 2007/8 (Palpacuer & Smith, 2021). These crises, such as the Rana Plaza incident in Bangladesh in 2013, the eruption of Covid-19, natural catastrophes, and Russia's 2022 invasion of Ukraine, have placed strain on conventional value chain structures (Fu, 2020; Gereffi, Posthuma, & Rossi, 2021; Dadush, 2022). Moreover, they may be creating cracks in the ability of the dominant socio-technical regime to maintain stability (Lund-Thomsen, 2022).

1.4.2 Key Actors in Sustainable Value Chain Innovation

A number of key actors can be identified as being involved in industrial and governance innovation for sustainability related to garment value chains, with the same actors often being involved in both. These can be broadly divided into firms, governments, and other social actors (Gereffi & Lee, 2016). The motivations of these actors can be shaped by multiple factors, such as the nature of the actor and where in the world they are located. While each actor can have a different perspective, it is also important to consider that collaboration and interaction between actors is a key element of innovation for sustainability (Riisgaard et al., 2020).

Firms involved in innovation can range from global brands to suppliers to other businesses connected to value chains. Innovation can occur as 'intrapreneurship', taking place within existing firms, or involve new start-ups. While firms are key actors in industrial innovation, they can also be involved in governance innovation, such as by setting supplier standards or participating in global governance forums.

Of course, government actors are key players in governance innovation. This process can involve agencies operating at the local, national, or international level. Governments can also play key roles in industrial innovation. For example, R&D can be carried out in public research institutes.

Finally, social actors are the most diverse group. This group can include civil society organisations and workers. Social actors often seek to play a governance role by creating pressures intended to shape the actions of businesses. This can be through pressuring businesses directly or seeking to change governance systems, such as by influencing government policy. Also, in some cases, social actors directly engage in industrial innovation. For example, NGOs sometimes found social enterprises (Lund-Thomsen, Lindgreen, & Vanhamme, 2016).

1.5 Contribution of the Element

Our Element is not the first work that discusses innovation that can help in integrating economic, environmental, and social concerns into core business processes. There is an emerging literature on business model innovation for sustainability (Maresova et al., 2022). This literature seeks to enable the integration of sustainability concerns within a firm's boundaries and in its interactions with external stakeholders through co-creation across decision levels and processes. Business models here refer to the cognitive structures that reflect the underlying logic of an existing or envisioned way of doing business. Business model innovations are then aimed at generating non-trivial or more systemic forms of innovation – in this case, related to business sustainability (Markovic & Tollin, 2021). In the context of this Element, the focus on the development of business models involving sustainability innovation is relevant to the extent that the current dominant system – that is, the fast-fashion model – is clearly not sustainable. Hence, there is a growing focus on creating a circular economy and 'slow fashion' business models, which could help in addressing some of the more unsustainable practices related to the industry's generation of waste. Some of the examples that we mention later in the Element refer to such attempts at finding alternative business models for sustainability within the industry (Rana & Allen, 2021).

However, in writing an Element about sustainable value chain innovation in the global garment industry, our concern is broader than what can be captured within a more firm-level focus on (un)sustainable business models. Adopting a GVC lens to sustainable innovation allows us to place such innovations within the broader structural context of volatile global markets, systemic inequalities in the distribution of costs and risks associated with GVC participation, and the unequal allocation of financial benefits resulting from product, process, and organisational forms of innovation in GVCs. In fact, it is often lead firms that generate the largest margins from new product or process innovations, even if these innovations may have been made by their own suppliers (Ponte, 2019). A case in point is the global football manufacturing industry, where branded buyers often have a small number of highly capable suppliers who compete among each other in terms of coming up with new product designs, production processes, and more eco-friendly forms of production. These suppliers also pay the development costs for these innovations. The branded buyers then promote these new products and can sell them with a price premium (Lund-Thomsen et al., 2012).

In this vein, our focus on sustainable value chain innovation is connected to literature on GVC upgrading (Giuliani, Pietrobelli, & Rabellotti, 2005; Barrientos, Gereffi, & Rossi, 2011; De Marchi et al., 2019). We share some common assumptions with the interlinked works on environmental upgrading in GVCs in a narrower sense and green industrialisation in a broader sense (Ponte, 2019; Jensen & Whitfield, 2022). For example, the environmental upgrading literature has been concerned with understanding how suppliers can environmentally upgrade through the production of less environmentally harmful products, the adoption of more environmentally-friendly and less resource-intensive production processes, and organisational upgrading that facilitates the implementation of environmental management systems within supplier firms (De Marchi et al., 2019; Khan, Ponte, & Lund-Thomsen, 2020). We also share concerns that have been raised that buyer-driven environmental upgrading, as well as buyer-driven social upgrading (i.e., making changes in order to be compliant with buyers' labour standards) happen within the overall context of a sustainability-driven supplier squeeze whereby global lead firms demand continuous price declines from their suppliers while insisting that their suppliers should pay the upgrading costs (Ruwanpura & Wrigley, 2011; Ponte, 2019). Overall, there is an unequal distribution of the costs, risks, and benefits associated with upgrading between lead firms and their suppliers in GVCs.

Undoubtedly, it is a fact that the so-called sustainability-driven supplier squeeze does exist, and this is a clear hindrance for ensuring a more economically just sustainability transition. However, in the context of this Element, we would also like to retain a somewhat more optimistic view of sustainable value chain innovation. Yes, the sustainability-driven supplier squeeze does exist. Yet, in spite of its existence, it is nevertheless remarkable just how many new ways of working with circularity principles, new forms of experimentation with raw materials, and new technologies are emerging within the context of GVCs. It is also remarkable just how many new actors have appeared in recent years with a specific mandate to engage in different forms of sustainable value chain innovation. Hence, while not denying the existence of unequal power relations between lead firms, suppliers, and workers in the global garment industry, our Element is dedicated to documenting the variety of new actors and forms of innovation that take place within the industry, in spite of these pre-existing systemic inequalities.

As discussed in Section 1.3.3, we also acknowledge the existence of a rich literature on innovation within GVCs. In particular, there has been a focus on the role that such chains can play in building and deepening the innovation capabilities of suppliers who participate in GVCs (Lema et al., 2019). A pessimistic picture emerged from early research on the potential for local suppliers to upgrade their innovation capabilities by learning from their interactions with global buyers in these chains. It was generally considered that lead firms would allow their suppliers to engage in inventing new products and processes through their GVC participation but that lead firms would not allow suppliers (in developing countries) to engage in chain upgrading – for instance, building their own brands in European and North American markets (Humphrey & Schmitz, 2002; Schmitz, 2006). However, recent cases have shown some examples of supplier firms overcoming this hurdle, particularly where state policy has been well-targeted (De Marchi & Alford, 2022). In a broader sense, the literature has highlighted that learning from GVC participation can vary significantly between suppliers and that their capacity to absorb, master, and adapt the knowledge and capabilities that lead firms can transfer to them also differs. However, the GVC and innovation literature often focuses on innovation driven by lead firms, thus leading to a poor conceptualisation of learning processes within suppliers in their own right (Lema, Rabellotti, & Sampath, 2018).

Furthermore, with ongoing global developments, the excessive focus on North American and European lead firms as sources of innovation in the global garment industry no longer seems to make sense. Key changes include the rise of increasingly large domestic markets in emerging economies such as China, India, and Pakistan and the growth of South–South trade (Horner & Nadvi, 2018). These changes have involved the establishment of many new clothing brands that cater to these expanding markets (Pasquali, Godfrey, & Nadvi, 2021).

Understanding innovation in GVCs also requires looking at innovation systems (Hekkert et al., 2007; Lundvall, 2016; Lema et al., 2018; De Marchi, Giuliani, & Rabellotti, 2018). We place our own understanding of sustainability innovation as linked to the access that firms may have to specialised skills, capital, extension services, standard certifications, incubation services, financial services, and other research inputs. While recognising that local innovation systems can certainly play a role in facilitating the development of innovation capabilities, we also believe that sustainability innovation in GVCs involves diverse global connections. Firms can connect to multiple scales of innovation systems within a larger global innovation system (Binz & Truffer, 2017). For instance, in the garment and textile industries, many large-scale suppliers in the Global South attend industry conferences across the world, are members of multi-stakeholder sustainability initiatives, directly hire global sustainability consultancy services, and/or tap into other global knowledge networks. These learning and innovation opportunities are often not directly linked to Northern lead firms, nor do they result directly from their interaction with other stakeholders in local innovation systems.

This Element also contributes to literature on sustainability innovation and sustainability transitions. We acknowledge that sustainability innovation can take multiple forms. Innovations can create or amplify sustainability challenges. Innovations can also involve supporting and building sustainable systems. Sustainability innovations involve 'blending economic, ecological, and social values' (Strambach, 2017, p. 501). Moreover, sustainability innovation is often connected to sustainable entrepreneurship. For market systems, commercially sustainable industrial innovation needs to involve a coincidence of private and social benefits. However, if these do not align, institutional entrepreneurship involving governance innovation related to changing regulations or market institutions can change the situation of the marketplace to make industrial innovations more viable (Schaltegger & Wagner, 2011).

As described in Section 1.3.1, innovation can lead to transitions, and as such, sustainability innovations can lead to sustainability transitions. These transitions, which involve large-scale societal changes that are needed to solve societal challenges (Loorbach, Frantzeskaki, & Avelino, 2017), can involve the co-evolution of multiple innovations which could bring together aspects such as technological, social, and institutional developments. Innovation within GVCs may play a critical role in future transitions. Notably, space has been identified as a key element to consider in relation to transitions. However, this topic is under-researched (Strambach, 2017). For countries to develop or adopt sustainability innovations that lead to broader transitions, sufficient local knowledge bases may be necessary, even when global connections exist. This need may make it more difficult for developing countries to undergo transition processes as it takes time to develop new knowledge bases (Strambach, 2017). Hence, future global level transitions need to address global inequalities that are often at the core of how value chains connect diverse production locations and processes.

Governance is also a key theme in this element. While sustainability transitions are complex processes, they can be governed (Kemp, Loorbach, & Rotmans, 2007; Nill & Kemp, 2009; Markand, Geels, & Raven, 2020; Van Mierlo & Beers, 2020). Governing sustainability transitions involves complex dynamics which span far beyond promoting innovation at the firm level (Loorbach et al., 2017). Notably, governance for sustainability transitions is a multi-actor process in which changes are developed through experimenting and learning. Transition governance involves promoting innovation as well as dealing with regime destabilisation and the emergence of new institutions that provide stability. Furthermore, shifting power relationships between governance actors have been found to be an inherent part of transition processes.

One aspect of governance related to sustainability transitions is the role of civil society groups. Social innovation by such groups can involve stimulating changes to popular beliefs, which can facilitate the development of a transition (Loorbach et al., 2017). Notably, visioning can be an important part of change processes. The process can involve motivating, coordinating, and empowering short- and medium-term action (Nevens et al., 2013).

Research has explored triggers for developing stronger policies to support sustainability transitions. Factors seen to have stimulated government action include shocks or crises, action by coalitions drawing attention to an issue, shifting public opinion, emerging feasibility of scaling niche technologies, and economic or socio-political regime destabilisation weakening previously existing resistance to new policies (Geels, 2019). However, it is important to note that policy makers can help to stimulate some of these conditions in the first place. Policy approaches, which can involve multi-stakeholder collaboration, can be considered on a spectrum from top-down steering to market models, which are designed to shape framework conditions in which other actors self-organise (Geels, 2019). Through such diverse strategies, policy actors can engage in governance innovation and stimulate industrial innovation, which can support transitions.

In short, focusing on the firm-level or even narrowly on the linkages between lead firms and suppliers in relation to sustainable value chain innovations may miss the forest for the trees. In many ways, sustainability innovations in value chains originate from a much broader set of actors than those that are directly involved in individual firms or buyer–supplier relations. For instance, technology providers, sustainability monitoring firms, and sustainability consultants may all have important functions in the development of sustainability innovation in value chains. Hence, in many ways, our Element emphasises the importance of taking a network approach. We seek to look beyond narrow forms of vertical value chain analysis to emphasise the many horizontal linkages and diverse connections that exist within the industry. We also highlight the roles of diverse 'sustainability innovators' whose unique knowledge and subject expertise feed into innovations in all parts of the network.

1.6 Element Overview

The rest of this Element is dedicated to providing an overview of sustainable value chain innovation related to the garment industry. Our focus is mainly on production practices. However, at some points we cover innovations related to the use and post-use phases of the product life cycle.

Within the overall structure of the Element, we acknowledge that the different forms of innovation that the sections describe are not mutually exclusive. Instead, they often overlap. Across the discussion, we seek to cover the diverse and intertwined forms of innovation that are taking place in various parts of the global garment industry and assess the landscape of innovation that is taking place around the world, critically assessing different approaches to sustainable value chain innovation.

In Section 2, we focus on governance innovation. On the one hand, we acknowledge that governance actors, such as lead firms or government agencies, as part of the socio-technical regime, may seek to promote current norms and ethical values in relation to value chain organisation. On the other, we also show that value chain governance actors have the ability to play roles in promoting change (Geels, 2004). Hence, we consider a variety of governance actors that seek to change industrial practices and some of the strategies that they have developed.

In Section 3, we move from a governance perspective to focussing on industrial innovation. Specifically, we consider incremental sustainability innovation that takes place within existing value chain structures. While these innovations can have substantial impacts in terms of addressing sustainability challenges at individual tiers of the chain, they do not necessarily challenge existing power relations within value chains nor those involving outside actors.

In Section 4, we explore emerging forms of radical industrial innovation. While we acknowledge that the distinction between incremental and radical innovation may not always be crystal clear, we contend that some forms of sustainability innovation may have greater potential to disrupt existing value chain relationships and structures. In particular, we outline new business models that could potentially have a disruptive effect and contribute to more sustainable garment production on a worldwide basis.

Finally, in the concluding section, Section 5, we consider how we can answer the five questions that we outlined at the beginning of this section. Additionally, we consider the implications of the material presented in this Element as it relates to future research, policy, and practice.

2 Governance Innovation

As discussed in Section 1, businesses' behaviours are often shaped by the dominant socio-technical regimes in which they operate. For value chains, these regimes can include actors within the chain, such as lead firms, and third parties, such as government agencies. For the most part, these governance actors maintain relative stability, which can restrict innovation. However, governance actors can also purposefully seek to promote changes to industrial practices. When taking new actions related to stimulating industrial change, governance actors can be seen to be engaging in processes of governance innovation. Governance in value chains can involve both direct and diffuse pressures (Dallas et al., 2019) – for example, attempts to change individual organisations' behaviour or seeking to change the dynamics of public discourse. This section considers how a diverse set of actors are creating innovative governance pressures related to addressing sustainability challenges in the garment industry or achieving the SDGs.

2.1 Governance within Value Chains

Actors within value chains have been developing a variety of ways to influence production processes related to sustainability. Key actors considered here are lead firms, producers, and workers. They can each have different priorities and different abilities to trigger change.

2.1.1 Lead Firms As Governance Actors

To address sustainability-related objectives, lead firms have been involved in concerted efforts to change the behaviour of actors in value chains, with a particular focus on their first-tier suppliers. Large brands and retailers' sustainability initiatives targeted at changing suppliers' behaviours emerged in the 1990s. These initiatives have evolved over the years.

When lead firms' sustainability-related supplier governance initiatives started, the dominant approach was based on a compliance paradigm, with buyers expecting suppliers to follow new sustainability standards (Lund-Thomsen & Lindgreen, 2014), which initially centered on codes of conduct related to factory workers. More recently, companies have been expanding the scope of their sustainability governance to include a broader range of issues and have been increasingly adopting approaches which fit within a cooperative paradigm, as well as exploring incentive-based approaches (Lund-Thomsen & Lindgreen, 2014; Alexander, 2020).

The compliance approach involves lead firms adopting standards, demanding suppliers adhere to these standards, monitoring supplier compliance with these standards, and excluding non-complying suppliers from their GVCs (Locke, 2013). This approach has been broadly criticised. Key problems are top-down structures, excluding the perspectives of local suppliers; audit fraud, including coaching of management and workers to fool auditors; and generation of multiple, sometimes contradictory, social and environmental requirements imposed on suppliers (Locke, Amengual, & Mangla, 2009).

The cooperation approach is often hailed as a more progressive strategy, involving the revising of buyer practices to provide suppliers with higher prices, longer lead times, and more stable trade relationships (Lund-Thomsen & Lindgreen, 2014). A cooperation strategy can involve supporting capacity development of supplier management and workers related to topics such as labour rights, worker entitlements, human resource management, and social dialogue participation. Furthermore, this approach can involve cooperation with local NGOs, trade unions, and multi-stakeholder initiatives. This approach has been praised as being a more credible way of gaining insights into the actual state of affairs within supplier factories. Yet the cooperation strategy has also been subject to critiques suggesting it is idealistic and unrealistic. Buyers tend to engage in a continuous price squeeze, and users of the cooperation approach often do not accept local supplier perspectives on sustainability but instead keep on enforcing buyer priorities – for instance, the eradication of child labour instead of the generation of local economic development and livelihoods (Lund-Thomsen, 2022).

It has been suggested that the compliance and cooperation approaches to sustainability in GVCs are often overlapping (Ghori et al., 2022). Ghori and co-authors have recently suggested that it may make more analytical sense to think of a 'hybrid' cooperation-compliance model of sustainability in GVCs. Here, the cooperation approach relates to buyers (or multi-stakeholder initiatives) cooperating with suppliers in ways where capacity-building measures precede and enable supplier compliance with corporate codes of conduct. Following capacity-building of local producers, compliance monitoring takes place, with the use of both traditional auditors and NGOs or trade unions. Hence, compliance measures are introduced to the extent that suppliers – which have received capacity-building measures and still do not comply with buyer codes of conduct – are given a limited time period to come into compliance – for instance, six months. If suppliers are still not in compliance after this grace period, lead firms then exclude them from their value chains.

A third approach is that buyers can also be involved in sustainable value chain innovation through designing mechanisms that shape market incentives. These incentives can function in an open market with buyers creating indirect types of incentives. For instance, brands and retailers have promoted benefits of best practices related to sustainability through developing and advertising freely available online learning resources related to improving environmental or social impacts during garment production processes (Alexander, 2020). Lead firms can also create direct incentives for supplier businesses. This approach was used by PUMA, a German sports company, which launched a programme in 2016 that was designed to incentivise suppliers to improve their sustainability performance (Sustainable Brands, 2016). The programme, which was carried out in partnership with the International Finance Corporation (IFC), gave suppliers access to loans with preferential funding conditions if they performed well in PUMA's regular supplier audits, which cover social, environmental, and health and safety components. Broadly speaking, there can also be overlap between the compliance and incentives approaches. When lead firms set sustainability-related standards for future purchases, they are creating incentives for potential future suppliers to adopt these standards.

Alternatively, incentive systems can operate internally within large businesses. An example of using a market incentive within a company can be found in the actions of Marks & Spencer, a British general retailer which sells private label clothing. The company set a goal of every product incorporating at least one sustainability attribute from a predefined list (Marks & Spencer, 2012). Staff were encouraged to be innovative in how to achieve this goal for each product. Additional incentives were created through incorporating sustainability targets as a factor shaping directors' annual bonuses. Furthermore, the company set up an innovation fund that was accessible to staff who developed ideas which could help the company meet its sustainability goals.

Another way that garment sector lead firms act as governance actors is through their roles in shaping global discourse. This can involve participating in policy dialogue as well as more directed efforts, such as lobbying governments related to policy (Oka, 2018). Through these types of actions, lead firms contribute to shaping the environment in which all value chain actors operate.

While garment sector lead firms typically operate as competitors, when it comes to playing roles related to governance for sustainability, they are increasingly becoming collaborators (Ashwin et al., 2020, Oka, Egels-Zandén, & Alexander, 2020). In some cases, collaboration can involve formal business associations. Business associations may exist specifically to address sustainability challenges or to promote broad-ranging mandates (Lund-Thomsen et al., 2016). Amfori is a Belgium-based business association with more than 2,400 members who are retailers, importers, brands, and associations from more than 40 countries (Amfori, n.d.). The association's mission is to enable organisations to enhance human prosperity, use natural resources responsibly, and drive open trade globally. Amfori provides its members with support on promoting socially and environmentally sustainable value chains and advocates on behalf of its members' interests.

Lead firm collaboration can also be less formal. For example, ad hoc working groups can be created to deal with emerging sustainability challenges. In some cases, such ad hoc groups can lead to collective action, as was the case in Cambodia in 2014. After several days of garment worker protests ended with military police shooting protesters, resulting in five deaths, more than thirty injured, and twenty-three union leaders being detained without trial, a group of global garment brands came together to respond (Oka, 2018). Initially, seven brands wrote a letter condemning the violence. Then, a few months later, a group of brand representatives went to Cambodia to meet with government representatives. These brands threatened to withdraw their orders from Cambodia. Eventually, facing this pressure, the government released the detained activists.

2.1.2 Producers As Governance Actors

While garment producers are often seen as creating sustainability challenges, they can also act as governance actors seeking to address sustainability challenges. First of all, producers' contributions to economic sustainability are often overlooked. In areas that suffer from issues such as lack of employment or poor infrastructure, economic investments into projects that can create jobs can be considered as addressing sustainability challenges.

One way that producers provide governance is by working through industry associations. As collective bodies, these associations can provide services to their members which assist with addressing challenges related to sustainable production. For example, the Bangladesh Garment Manufacturers and Exporters Association (BGMEA) has supported its members with running several projects related to reducing their environmental impact (BGMEA, 2021). Industry associations can also play a role in seeking to improve local infrastructure where production takes place, such as supporting the development of common effluent treatment plants that are used for treating liquid waste from production facilities (Yoon & Nadvi, 2018).

Additionally, another way that producers in garment value chains can support governance for sustainable production is through participating in multi-stakeholder coalitions. This involvement can be through industry associations or also involve individual producers joining coalitions. Through participating in international coalitions, these actors can help to shape the global discourse surrounding sustainability in the garment industry.

2.1.3 Unions and Workers As Governance Actors

Unions and workers have also used innovative practices to seek to directly and indirectly (e.g., participating in global discourse) shape the behaviours of garment industry firms. A key innovation has been unions moving beyond their traditional roles of building agreements between workers and their direct employers to develop a variety of transnational industrial relations agreements which are targeted at shaping behaviour in value chains (Ashwin et al., 2020). These agreements have taken multiple forms.

One approach unions have used is developing global framework agreements (GFAs). These agreements are negotiated at the global level between unions and individual lead firms. They are intended to protect workers' interests across multinational operations. Issues incorporated can include health, safety, and environmental practices. In 2007, the International Textile, Garment and Leather Workers' Federation (ITGLWF) signed the first GFA in the garment sector with Inditex, a large Spanish fashion company (Miller, 2011).

Unions have also developed multi-brand agreements. The garment sector has seen the development of several such initiatives. The Accord on Fire and Building Safety in Bangladesh (n.d.) is a prominent example. This initiative involved an agreement between two unions and more than 200 lead firms which sought to promote health and safety in the garment and textile industries in Bangladesh. Furthermore, unions also shape global discourse.

In cases where workers are not organised in unions, they can still take action to address sustainability challenges. This can even occur where workers are in challenging circumstances (Li, 2021; Mieres & McGrath, 2021). Notably, in Vietnam, where strikes are illegal and trade unions do not organise them, garment workers have frequently engaged in wildcat strikes, organised at the workplace level. Through these actions, Vietnamese workers have been able to achieve a variety of demands (Anner, 2015).

2.2 Public Policy

In addition to actors within value chains, another important category of actors to consider related to governance for sustainability in the garment industry is public sector agencies. A wide range of public policies are being developed to promote responsible business practices. Examples include those related to reporting, trade agreements, taxes, bribery and corruption, socially responsible investment, the environment, labour, and human rights (OECD, 2020). Policies can be categorised in different ways. One dimension is whether they use hard or soft mechanisms. Related to value chains, LeBaron and Rühmkorf (2017) propose that policies can be considered as spanning a range from softest to hardest, with examples of softer approaches including transparency legislation and harder approaches involving due diligence liabilities. Another dimension is whether they focus on standards or promote actions beyond the minimum requirements of the law (Steurer, Margula, & Martinuzzi, 2012).

Challenges related to sustainable production in value chains typically involve activities that cross through multiple locations. Consequently, public regulation of production can be a difficult process. Regulators working at different scales (e.g., local, national, regional, and global) have developed diverse policies and interventions which are intended to promote sustainable production. An important factor to consider is that individual value chain actors can be covered by layers of multi-scalar governance (Alford, Barrientos, & Visser, 2017). The discussion that follows considers tactics that have been used across governance scales.

2.2.1 Local

Problems related to sustainable production are often felt strongly at a local scale. For example, air pollution from a factory may be experienced locally or communities may face challenges related to working conditions within that factory. Local governments can create laws and run programmes which seek to address sustainability challenges occurring within their jurisdictions (Lund-Thomsen et al., 2016).

A key challenge for local governments is that some localities have a situation in which many people are employed by one dominant employer or industry. This can create conflicts of interest for local regulators related to promoting economic interests of constituents while supporting social and environmental sustainability. For example, a community in South India with a large textile dyeing industry faced decades of legal challenges driven by different groups in relation to tensions between the economic benefits of business-as-usual versus taking action to address a growing water pollution problem. In the end, new regulations were put in place which encouraged the development of technologically advanced effluent treatment facilities (Alexander, 2021). Another challenge can be that local governments may not have the power to directly control practices that are of concern. Consequently, local actors may need to be innovative when seeking to design feasible initiatives that can address local sustainability challenges.

2.2.2 National

Production practices are often regulated at a national level. National policies can impact multinational enterprises in multiple ways. Different policies can be applied by their home countries, their subsidiaries' host countries, and any other countries where they operate. For example, a large garment manufacturer, such as the Hong Kong–based Crystal group, is subject to laws governing production practices in the five countries where they operate.

One aspect of national regulations is shaping dynamics of practices used by domestic businesses. Another aspect is setting conditions that may be intended to attract foreign direct investment. A tactic which has been used by many countries for the latter purpose is to create export processing zones, regions with regulations that differ from the rest of the country and are often designed to appeal to foreign investors. These zones have often been seen as places that are prone to sustainability challenges. However, in some cases, governments have engaged in sustainability innovation related to how they are set up. For example, the Ethiopian government has built eco-industrial parks as part of its national industrialisation strategy (Jensen & Whitfield, 2022).

In addition to governing production practices, governments can regulate what happens with clothing items during and after their use stage. At the use stage, this can include regulations such as efficiency of washing machines. For the post-use stage, France, for example, has developed an extended producer responsibility scheme for clothing which has been in place since 2006 (Šajn, 2019).

Policies that are focussed on promoting corporate responsibility have been called CSR policies. National CSR policies have been considered as ranging in their levels of maturity (Martinuzzi, Krumay, & Pisano, 2011). The most advanced countries can be seen to have a 'CSR Strategy', followed by, in decreasing levels of maturity, a 'CSR Action Plan', then the use of individual CSR policy instruments or frameworks that shape understandings of CSR.

National CSR approaches have been considered as having three key elements (Martinuzzi et al., 2011). The first element is the objectives. The second is the choice of policy instruments, which can include diverse mechanisms such as command-and-control, economic/market-based, voluntary instruments, information-based instruments, feedback mechanisms, as well as hybrid and network components. The third element is the type of governance structure (i.e., type of coordination between political-administrative actors and other stakeholders). This structure can involve horizontal integration (between national-level actors) or vertical integration (between national and sub-national actors) and the use of indicators, monitoring mechanisms, and qualitative evaluation.

Another way to classify CSR public policies was developed by Knudsen, Moon, and Slager (2015). Their framework draws on Fox, Ward, and Howard (2002) to identify four types of CSR policies (mandate, facilitate, partner, and endorse). Each policy can be considered as having a range of regulatory strengths, breadths of issue application, and levels of institutionalisation.

Finally, another issue to consider is that, within a national government, different roles can be played by different ministries or departments (Fransen, 2013). Globally, there are high levels of variation on how national sustainability policies and strategies are organised. For example, in 2000, the UK was the first country to appoint a Minister for Corporate Social Responsibility (Idowu & Schmidpeter, 2015).

2.2.3 International

Additionally, some forms of regulation operate at an international level. These often involve national governments agreeing to collaborative objectives, guidelines, or plans. International public sector regulation can take a number of forms. For instance, the EU is in the process of enacting various legislative frameworks, such as the Corporate Sustainability Reporting Directive and the Corporate Sustainability Due Diligence Directive, which will have implications for how brands, retailers, and suppliers address sustainability issues in the global garment industry (Euronext, 2022).

Regional agreements make up one form of international governance that can shape production practices. For example, the 1998 MERCOSUR[2] Social and Labour Declaration recognises declarations concerning human rights and civil and political freedoms, which cover topics such as non-discrimination, protection of migrant and cross-border workers, forced labour, child labour, freedom of association, trade union freedom, unemployment protection, vocational training, occupational health and safety, labour inspection, and the right to social security (Siroën, 2013). Another example is the EU ecolabel. This labeling system is a voluntary certification that involves ecological criteria for clothing, which is an incentive to improve production standards (Šajn, 2019).

International governance can also be at a global scale. One key global initiative was mentioned in the Introduction (Section 1), the SDGs. Another

---

[2] MERCOSUR (the Southern Common Market) is a regional integration process that was established by Argentina, Brazil, Paraguay, and Uruguay and subsequently joined by Venezuela and Bolivia.

major global governance mechanism is the OECD Guidelines for Multinational Enterprises (OECD, 2019). The guidelines form an international legal instrument that provides standards related to responsible business conduct that cover human rights, labour rights, the environment, bribery, consumer interest, information disclosure, science and technology, competition, and taxation. A key element of the OECD's approach is that companies should engage in risk-based due diligence. The guidelines have been adopted by all OECD members (thirty-eight countries) as well as twelve interested non-OECD members.

National and international government agencies have sought to regulate global production practices by creating mechanisms which can shape production practices of items that are imported into their countries or regions or are connected to the operation of domestically operating firms.[3] These regulations are often focussed on creating obligations for lead firms in value chains. One example can be found in the UK. To address concerns that modern slavery was happening in connection to the practices of businesses that were operating in the country, the national government developed the Modern Slavery Act 2015.[4] This act covers companies operating in the UK with an annual turnover of more than 36 million GBP which supply goods or services. It stipulates that firms meeting these criteria have to publish a report outlining the practices they have undertaken to address modern slavery within their business and in their supplier base. The law does not regulate what actions the companies need to take but seeks to use the reputational impact the reports would have in order to push firms into taking action to prevent modern slavery in their own practices and in their value chain operations that take place globally. Other examples of similar regulations can be found in Australia's Modern Slavery Act, France's Corporate Duty of Vigilance Law, and regulation that is being developed at the EU level. Another approach that importing countries can use is to create regulations intended to support manufacturing countries' laws (Bartley, 2018).

A number of laws also regulate garment and textile waste, which can flow across national borders. Many countries now export used clothing in high levels. In some cases, this can disrupt domestic clothing industries by creating low-priced second-hand clothing markets that can outcompete domestic production. As a result, countries, such as India and Nigeria, have developed policies banning imports of used clothing (Brooks, 2019). Facing barriers on exporting waste, governments are developing new strategies. For example, the

---

[3] A number of articles explore this type of law (see Knudsen, et al., 2015; LeBaron & Rühmkorf, 2017; Smit et al., 2020).

[4] Modern slavery is defined by the UK government as 'slavery, servitude and forced or compulsory labour; and human trafficking' (see *Transparency in Supply Chains etc: A Practical Guide*, Guidance issued under section 54(9) of the Modern Slavery Act 2015).

European Commission has been involved in promoting the development of new laws related to managing textile waste (Šajn, 2019). Member states are expected to develop systems to collect textile waste by 2025.

2.3 Other Types of Governance Actors

A variety of other third-party actors are also seeking to change the incentives of value chain actors. These organisations can be specialised to focus on sustainability in garment value chains or have broader missions. They include NGOs and support service providers, as well as other actors.

2.3.1 NGOs

Globally, there are many NGOs with missions related to promoting a sustainable garment industry. These organisations have a variety of foci. Some are dedicated to addressing a small-scale local sustainability challenge within a community and others have global ambitions. These organisations often develop multiple projects and innovative ways to try to promote the causes they support.

One focus that NGOs have had related to influencing garment production processes is trying to influence the behaviour of lead firms in value chains. To achieve this aim, NGOs have developed a wide variety of tactics. Such appeals have often involved name and shame campaigns. Notably, in the 1990s, the US-based National Labor Committee ran campaigns that publicly put the spotlight on poor labour practices in the value chains of brands including The Gap and Disney (Bartley & Child, 2014). In addition, NGOs have developed collaborative approaches. These involve partnering with lead firms to develop new policies and programmes. Collaborative NGO approaches can be seen in the actions of some organisations promoting a living wage in Southeast Asia (Ford & Gillan, 2021). Moreover, NGOs are involved in a variety of other activities that are targeted directly at influencing suppliers in GVCs. These activities can also take different forms. For example, they can work with suppliers to provide support services for their workers. Finally, another key governance role played by NGOs is contributing to public debates. In this role, NGOs often create public reports and participate in global forums related to shaping the regime that governs the garment industry. Through such actions, they can change the environment in which businesses operate.

Some NGOs take the form of multi-stakeholder organisations, which have contributions from a diverse group of other organisations (Fransen & Burgoon, 2014; De Bakker, Rasche, & Ponte, 2019). Examples include the Ethical Trade Initiative and the Fair Wear Foundation. Multi-stakeholder initiatives can play multiple roles in value chains, which include providing learning platforms, developing standards, developing enforcement mechanisms, and issuing labels and certifications (Searcy, Kapuscinski, & Dooley, 2017). While these organisations have the benefit of bringing diverse perspectives together, some have been criticised for failing to effectively balance the needs of all stakeholders (Soundararajan, Brown, & Wicks, 2019).

2.3.2 Support Service Providers

Actions by support service providers can change the competitive dynamics of the markets where garment firms work. For example, the spread of private (and voluntary public) sustainability standards has created competitive pressure for garment brands and retailers to adopt these standards. Funders can also promote sustainable innovation. An example can be found in REFASHIOND Ventures, a supply chain venture fund which seeks to invest in companies that are rethinking supply chains ((E) BrandConnect, 2020).

2.3.3 Other Actors

Other actors that can play governance roles include media actors and educators. For example, media organisations, individuals producing content on social media, and educators can shape perceptions and behaviours of consumers. These actors can play diffuse roles that shape norms and expectations.

2.4 Limitations for Different forms of Governance

While this section has shown that innovation within governance actors is diverse, it is important to remember that the main governance pressures within the garment industry promote stability. All of these governance initiatives intended to promote change related to sustainability are experienced by target groups in a context where they feel multiple pressures to maintain current practices. However, current events may be creating cracks in the stabilising force of the overall governance regime. These circumstances may present an opportunity for innovative governance initiatives to create higher levels of impact.

Governance innovation involves using diverse tactics. Some approaches work by creating voluntary incentives for producers and lead firms. However, this type of approach faces specific challenges. One is that the worst performers may be less likely to respond if they know they will not be able to compete on issues such as sustainability-related marketing. This dynamic can limit impacts as changes may not reach businesses responsible for creating the most severe problems.

Another challenge of voluntary initiatives is that companies can receive reputational benefits through publicly joining them, while actually continuing to use a variety of actions which perpetuate sustainability challenges. Additionally, third parties can have an incentive to keep their members happy and continue to receive membership fees. This incentive structure can prevent certain sustainability issues from being addressed, or even publicly discussed, which is often the case with garment production taking place in countries that restrict workers' freedom of association.

Other governance activities more directly seek to control behaviours of value chain actors. This type of governance is typically played by government agencies but can also be played by other actors such as lead firms having high levels of control over suppliers or private organisations acting as industry regulators. These approaches can be limited as businesses can find multiple ways to evade regulation, which include compromising (making strategic changes), avoiding (ignoring the requirement), defying (resisting in a public way), and manipulating (finding a way around the requirement) (Oliver, 1991).

Alternately, some governance activities create diffuse pressures or incentives which aim to change the public discourse and stimulate innovation. Such governance can be diverse, ranging from formal reports to individuals posting content on social media. This type of action can have an influence but impacts can be difficult to directly observe.

With all of these governance initiatives, the aim is to change the behaviours of other actors. Some initiatives can be well targeted and lead to their desired changes, while others may miss their mark. When change happens, it can involve innovation within the organisations that are changing as well as the creation of new businesses. The next two sections consider types of sustainability-related industrial innovation that are taking place within value chains and creating new value chains.

3 Incremental and Firm-Level Process and Product Innovation

Industrial innovation can result from pressures created by governance systems, such as those that were discussed in Section 2. It can also emerge through other drivers, such as a desire to resolve sustainability challenges, a reaction to market demand, and the potentially destabilising effects of the multiple crises that have been impacting value chain structures. Additionally, it can emerge through chance. This section and Section 4 consider various forms of sustainability-related industrial innovation. All of the examples of innovation that will be discussed have taken place while the garment industry experiences strong pressures for stability created by the dominant socio-technical regime.

This section focusses on incremental innovation. As discussed in Section 1, incremental innovation involves small changes to existing products and processes. A key example is optimisation of existing processes. This is a type of innovation that can function within existing value chain structures, which does not present serious challenges to the socio-technical regime. Incremental innovation can occur through changes that take place within existing businesses as well as those that emerge through the creation of start-ups.

Incremental innovation can involve processes and products. Processes that are used within companies in value chains are often responsible for creating sustainability challenges. For example, problematic supervision systems can create poor working conditions. Developing innovative new processes can help to address ongoing challenges. In terms of processes, this section particularly focusses on innovation related to practices that are used within organisations. More radical changes to processes that involve how organisations interact with each other are considered in Section 4.

Product characteristics can also create sustainability challenges. As with processes, product innovation can be used to address ongoing challenges. However, it is important to note that developing a product innovation is a more outward-facing change than what is often involved in process innovation. A business with a product innovation needs to have customers for the new product. Another key aspect to consider about product innovation is that changing the qualities of a product can often involve changing production processes. Hence, product innovation often also involves process innovation.

Product innovation can include goods or services, which are both components of garment value chains. Physical products include the materials that go into a final garment (e.g., raw materials, buttons, and fabrics) as well other elements of production processes, such as machines and chemicals. Services in garment value chains are diverse. A range of services are bought by producers, lead firms, and final customers, as well as those related to garments' post-use phase. These services can be carried out by businesses, government agencies, and NGOs. Addressing sustainability challenges can involve modifying existing goods and services as well as creating new types of goods and services that may be specifically targeted at sustainability-related outcomes.

Across this section, diverse examples of incremental innovation are shared. The next three sub sections separately discuss innovation related to processes, physical product design, and service design. The conclusion to the section considers challenges and key dynamics related to each of these types of innovation.

3.1 Production and Post-Production Processes

Changes to production and post-production processes can reduce problematic outcomes related to conventional practices. As discussed in Section 1, garment production, use, and disposal involves diverse processes that are associated with sustainability challenges. Related to many of these challenges, diverse forms of innovation have been taking place.

Process upgrading can include factors such as the type of energy that is used in a factory and how waste is managed. A company that has improved the environmental impact of its production practices by using cleaner production techniques is Nova Textiles in Romania. This company changed the way that it cleans and bleaches its products and was able to save 73 per cent of chemical auxiliary consumption, 50 per cent of water consumption, 36 per cent of electrical energy consumption, 46 per cent of thermal energy consumption, 2,500 t/year in CO_2 emissions, and 50 per cent of effluent costs (Dumitrescu, Mocioiu, & Visileanu, 2008).

As most lead firms do not engage directly in production practices, there are some limitations to their ability to innovate in this area. Nevertheless, there are some ways that they can. One issue is that lead firms can have limited visibility of production processes that are used in their products. This can be a serious challenge for buyers as the processes being used may not leave any evidence in the final product that they receive. To address this issue, buyers can monitor production practices and, in some cases, buyers have developed targeted methods for attempting to shape their suppliers' processes as was discussed in Section 2. Another way that lead firms can incorporate better processes is through supplier choices. As also discussed in Section 2, many lead firms now assess potential suppliers to see if they follow a set of sustainability criteria. Additionally, another relevant supplier-related decision is location, which can influence many factors, including transportation processes. However, the most direct way that buyers are involved in process innovation is through the role they play in designing products. This is discussed more in Section 3.2.

Production equipment providers can also play a role in supporting process innovation. These are companies that make the equipment that producers use to make garment components and final garments. A number of these firms have recently been developing production technology that is designed to help with sustainability challenges, such as equipment that can reduce fabric waste at the cutting stage. Additionally, digital production monitoring technologies are being developed which can have sustainability-related benefits. For example, sensors have been developed to monitor levels of cotton dust, which can cause serious health problems, on the factory floor (Sutradhar et al., 2021).

3.2 Design of Physical Products

Product design is connected to sustainability in multiple ways. As discussed earlier in this section, product innovation can overlap with process innovation. Notably, product design is connected to risks during production practices. Another issue that is important to consider is that product design can shape use and post-use processes, such as recycling options.

Sustainability innovation in garment and textile design can involve multiple actors. Key actors involved in garment design include fashion designers (based at brands and retailers, design service providers, or manufacturers) and manufacturers of garments and component parts. Additional actors, such as product standard creators (public or private organisations), play a governance role in shaping design options, as was discussed in Section 2.

At a fundamental level, garment design includes choosing the material components and elements of how they are manipulated during the manufacturing process. Product designs can be very complex and can include many component parts, such as for a winter coat with many embellishments, or be very simple, such as a cotton T-shirt. In some cases, lead firms have detailed knowledge of all of the components in a product. However, this is rare in the garment industry. Lead firms may deal with a sourcing firm that acts as an intermediary in communications with first-tier producers and further down there are often limited connections and information flowing between each stage of garment production (Alexander, 2022).

All components of garments can be associated with sustainability challenges. In order to reduce risks of contributing to sustainability challenges, designers can exclude products which are associated with high levels of sustainability risks or can seek to include components which have defined sustainability criteria, such as products bearing a sustainability certification.

The garment design process can specifically consider the types of risks that may be more likely to be faced during production activities. For example, when a large-scale retailer or brand offers very intricate products, production activities, such as beading, may be likely to be carried out by home-based workers. While home-based work is not a problem in and of itself, it can be associated with risks. For example, home workers can be subject to problematic working conditions, such as piecework payments being lower than legal minimum wages (von Broembsen, 2020).

When particular production practices are known to create high risk of health or environmental damage, lead firms can use design to try to address these risks. One option is that companies can ban features which require such practices. This has been the case with sandblasting, a technique that has been used on denim to give it a worn-in look. The process can involve workers spraying sand at high pressure onto fabric, an activity that has been associated with causing silicosis, a condition in which the lungs are damaged through inhaling small particles (Riddselius, 2010). To prevent the risk of this practice being used in their value chains, in 2010 Levi Strauss & Co. and H&M, two major sellers of jeans, announced that they would ban sandblasting in all of their product lines (Levi Strauss, 2010).

Product innovation for sustainability can change the way the product functions or can address sustainability impacts without affecting how the product is used. For example, a product can use a material with similar attributes but that is more environmentally friendly. This could involve features such as being biodegradable or recyclable or being made from alternative substances that have fewer toxic components. For instance, PrimaLoft has produced a product called Bio which is a synthetic clothing insulation material that is made from recycled content and is completely recyclable and biodegradable (Tiernan, 2019). This provides an alternative to synthetic filling materials that are commonly used and take hundreds of years to break down.

Alternatively, innovation can change the features of final products. Changes of this sort could involve features such as the feel or appearance of a textile, the length of time a product lasts, or the ways in which the product can be used. An example is S.Café, a textile created by Singtex, a Taiwanese company. Made from coffee grounds, it dries more quickly than cotton and can be composted after use (Carrasco Rozas, 2017).

Product design can also shape sustainability challenges during a product's use. Energy requirements (during production, use, and disposal) are a key element of products' sustainability that is shaped by design as energy generation can create high levels of CO_2 emissions, which are a major contributor to climate change (Fecht, 2021). In terms of garment use, energy demand is related to how often items are washed and the type of washing they require. An example of related innovation is that textile treatments can be applied to fabrics to prevent the development of odour-causing bacteria, meaning that they need to be washed less often.

Furthermore, products can also create harmful by-products during their use, which is another problem that innovative companies can try to address during the design stage. In the garment sector, a topic that has recently received growing attention is the shedding of plastic microfibres during garment use. The Microfiber Innovation Challenge organised by Conservation X Labs with support from several companies (Under Armour, Finisterre, and Bolt Threads) as well as NGOs (Fashion for Good, Canopy, and Microfibre Consortium) sought to promote innovation related to reducing harm from microplastic pollution (Remington, 2022). Twelve product innovations were selected as finalists, which ranged from Werewool Fibers, which has a product that uses microorganisms to biosynthesise proteins that mimic natural materials, to Orange Fiber, which creates sustainable fabrics from the by-products of citrus juice (Microfiberinnovation, 2023).

The design stage is also a crucial factor in shaping the options for a garment's post-use life. Some materials can biodegrade or be recycled, while others have limited post-life uses and may end up in landfills or polluting waterways.[5] A key issue related to design and garments' post-use lives is the choice of materials. Companies can choose biodegradable or easily recycled materials or they can choose materials that are not easy to recycle or those which may be dangerous during the post-use phase. Many new biodegradable materials are being developed, such as textiles created by living organisms (Cirino, 2018).

Another issue related to design that shapes what can be done with a product after its use is how easily its component parts can be separated. Some design processes involve attaching materials in ways that are difficult to separate and make even recyclable components very difficult to recover. To help address such sustainability challenges, companies can take this into consideration in their design processes. For example, Resortecs is a Belgian company that has developed a process for creating clothing that can be easy to dissemble. They produce melting stitching thread, which allows for easy recovery of separate parts.

The design of garments' component parts is a key element of sustainability innovation. Producers acting as suppliers in GVCs can offer products with particular sustainability-related features. For example, product innovation can include offering denim made with recycled fibres. Usha Yarns in India sells a recycled denim yarn with 80 per cent of the content being cotton recovered from discarded denim waste and the other 20 per cent derived from recycled plastic bottles.

Product innovation at the producer level can also involve developing new substances to treat fabrics, such as dyes and other chemicals. For example, Archroma, a Swiss company, offers a dye called EarthColors. This dye is made from non-edible agriculture and agricultural waste products, which can help with addressing environmental and health related sustainability challenges.

Another element of physical product design for garments is packaging. Single-use plastics are a very common way to package products, which often creates high levels of waste that is not recyclable or is not recycled. Additionally, excessive packaging can take up more space during shipping processes, which can be associated with high CO_2 emissions related to transportation. To address this challenge, several companies have developed

---

[5] Section 4 has further discussion on businesses that take previously discarded post-use items and turn them into new products.

sustainable packaging options for the garment industry. For example, Paptic, a Finish company, has developed a recyclable and reusable packaging option.

3.3 Design of Services

As mentioned in Section 1, the range of services bought and sold within garment value chains is wide. These include conventional production-related services as well as emerging sustainability-focussed services. These new types of services can be targeted to producers and lead firms during garment production processes as well as to end consumers. These services can be provided by businesses, governments, and not-for-profit organisations. They have a range of functions that include providing standards and auditing, tracing services, capacity-building services, consulting services, and consumer-facing communications. In some cases, these services are provided by new entrepreneurial businesses and in others they have been developed within larger organisations through processes of intrapreneurship.

3.3.1 Production Services

Across production processes, producers can buy production services, such as dyeing or other fabric treatments. Often these service providers are considered as subcontractors in garment value chains and have been associated with informal contracts and a lack of regulation. They are often considered as a high risk element of the value chain. However, these businesses can also be innovative. For example, in India an embroidery initiative was developed with support from The Gap, an NGO, a sourcing intermediary, two factories, and a government agency, which helped individual home-based embroiderers connect to GVCs with better terms of trade (Tewari, 2017). Through this initiative, designs requiring hand-stitched embroidery could be created with lower risk of poor working conditions.

3.3.2 Intermediary Services and Logistics

The processes through which component parts and final products are traded, stored, and transported can also be responsible for creating multiple sustainability challenges. For example, these can range from trade intermediaries actively hiding problematic practices to transportation generating pollution. To address sustainability challenges, intermediaries and logistics providers have also been engaging in sustainable value chain innovation.

Value chains often involve numerous intermediaries, which can connect diverse buyers and suppliers (Serdijn, Kolk, & Fransen, 2020). Intermediaries can be microbusinesses which involve one person or they can be large companies. These firms play key roles related to sustainability issues, with functions including selecting factories to carry out production and being conduits for sharing lead firms' sustainability requirements (Soundararajan & Brammer, 2018). In these roles, the intermediaries can bridge differences between buyers and suppliers through translating expectations (Soundararajan, Khan, & Tarba, 2018).

In some cases, intermediaries have developed specific services related to promoting sustainable production. Examples of such services can involve arranging for producers to get sustainability-related certification, ensuring suppliers are chosen that have sustainability credentials and contributing to multi-stakeholder organisations' activities. An example of a garment sourcing firm that has sustainability at its core is Ethical and Sustainable Sourcing, a business that operates out of the USA and Canada and which specialises in sourcing clothing from Bangladesh.

Transportation and logistics can create key sustainability challenges in value chains. Transportation in value chains can involve road vehicles, trains, boats, and planes. Businesses in this industry are diverse. They range from truck owner-operators to large multinational logistics firms that coordinate global multimodal shipping arrangements.

Many sustainability campaigns related to transportation focus on identifying carbon emissions. Responding to increasing concerns with transportation-related emissions, some companies have changed the technologies used in shipping. For instance, A.P. Moller-Maersk, a container logistics company operating in 130 countries, provides carbon-neutral ocean shipping ((E) BrandConnect, 2020). This service is being used by H&M, a Swedish fashion brand.

Poor working conditions are also a concern in the logistics industry. In a 2019 survey with responses from sixty-nine managers working in European road transport, social and working conditions in international transport were described as deteriorating by 68 per cent of respondents (Vitols & Voss, 2019). The majority (79 per cent) described competition based on unfair practices and social dumping as the most important trends in the road freight transport business.[6] Sustainability innovation intended to address these challenges includes actions such as developing codes of conduct which outline workers' rights and creating whistle-blower programmes.

Another key issue is that drivers face health and safety risks due to long hours which can cause fatigue. Several companies have developed technology that can help drivers to prevent fatigue-related accidents. Optalert, an Australian company, has developed glasses that can help to prevent accidents during transport. These glasses monitor eye movements and inform drivers when signs of fatigue appear.

---

[6] Social dumping can involve hiring workers from lower-wage countries and giving contracts that do not have the same benefits as those provided to domestic workers.

The company describes the glasses as being able to predict drowsiness up to fifteen to twenty minutes prior to the onset of performance failure.

3.3.3 Sustainability Standards and Auditing

Adding to the longstanding forms of intermediaries, a number of new sustainability-focused intermediaries have been emerging. One area where this has occurred is creating and implementing sustainability standards and auditing systems. The world has seen an explosion of voluntary sustainability standards being developed by both public and private sector organisations (see Nadvi, 2014; Langford, 2019; Fransen, Kolk, & Rivera-Santos, 2019; Marques, 2019; Krauss & Krishnan, 2022) using diverse processes (Strambach & Surmeier, 2018). These standards can have a variety of impacts that include reducing harmful impacts and contributing to local capability-building (Surmeier, 2020).

Many sustainability standards are supported by third-party auditing firms. This has created a space for innovation in the auditing industry. Existing auditing firms have added sustainability-related services and new firms have emerged to focus on this area. One such example is Social Compliance Services Asia, a Hong Kong–based firm that certifies compliance with social standards. It has a team of auditors who work across multiple Asian countries and is affiliated with multiple global standards organisations.

3.3.4 Traceability Services

A second new type of sustainability-focussed service is provided by companies that offer to help lead firms trace the details of their value chains. As discussed in Section 1, many garment firms do not have high levels of knowledge of what is happening in the lower tiers of their value chains. A growing number of companies have been created to provide services and technology related to traceability. Technological-based innovation has been common in this area. Companies have been developing systems that use technology such as block chain, DNA tracing, chemical tracing, and radio-frequency identification (RFID), among others. For example, FibreTrace is an Australian company that has developed a technology that embeds luminescent pigments into fibres (Doyle, 2021). When these fibres are made into yarns and textiles, these pigments can be identified with a handheld scanner.

3.3.5 Capacity-Building Support

A third type of sustainability-focussed service is providing capacity-building support, such as training. While, as was discussed in Section 2, brands and retailers can provide capacity building for their suppliers, a variety of organisations have also emerged to provide sustainability-related capacity building services. Capacity building can be related to supporting suppliers in relation to meeting standards or can have broader aims, such as women's empowerment. Organisations providing such services can be commercial enterprises, not-for-profit organisations, or governments. These organisations can be based in and focus on individual countries or have international operations. An example of this type of training can be found in BSR's HERfinance programme (Goldenberg, 2014). This global programme, which is typically arranged by lead firms for supplier factories, involves training workers on financial literacy.

A specific form of capacity-building initiative that has been developed by private and public sector actors is business case sustainability initiatives (Oka, Egels-Zandén, Rahman, & Alexander, 2020). The key element of such programmes is their promise to help producers to make changes that result in their businesses being more profitable while also addressing a sustainability challenge. One such programme is the Bangladesh Partnership for Cleaner Textile (PaCT), which is led by IFC and involves support from the Embassy of Denmark, the Embassy of the Kingdom of the Netherlands, and the BGMEA, along with a variety of lead firms. The PaCT programme seeks to promote cleaner production practices that reduce waste and decrease production costs. The programme is offered on a voluntary basis to garment and textile factories.

3.3.6 Sustainability Consulting

A fourth type of sustainability-focussed service is sustainability consulting. Third parties have created a wide variety of business consulting services which can help to address sustainability challenges in value chains. Services offered include producing sustainability reports, developing sustainability plans, managing value chain engagement, and supporting the development of sustainable product design. Sustainability-focussed consulting services have been developed within existing consulting companies and new consulting companies have been founded with sustainability as their core mission. For example, Matrec is an Italian consulting and research company that specialises in sustainability and the circular economy. It has a lab that identifies sustainable materials, and it helps companies to incorporate new materials. Its clients include major global fashion brands.

3.3.7 Consumer-Facing Communication

Finally, a fifth type of sustainability-related service is providing consumer-facing communication. Notably, demand for lead firm transparency is growing from consumers and civil society groups as well as through emerging public regulation. Increasing visibility into production practices can help with identifying and remedying problematic situations. Responding to these incentives, lead firms have begun offering information about sustainability as a new service they provide for customers. In addition, a range of organisations now offer lead firms help with sustainability-related communications.

Specifically, lead firms have increasingly been publishing a variety of reports which provide different forms of information about their value chains. Connected to the growth of traceability initiatives, many fashion brands and retailers have begun to publish information on their first-tier suppliers (Schüßler et al., 2018). In addition, some companies have begun to publish the names of businesses involved in parts of their lower-tier supplier bases. Innovation has also been taking place related to how brands and retailers share information. In an effort to improve transparency, Asket, a Swedish clothing retailer, provides customers with impact receipts. These receipts outline levels of CO_2, water, and energy use involved in making each product. Another company that has been developing more transparent practices is Able, a US-based fashion company that produces bags, clothes, shoes, and jewellery. Their brand has a mission to support women workers around the world. They work closely with producers to provide better jobs. They publish the wages of workers at their production facilities in the USA and Ethiopia and are in the process of collecting the data to publish information about their suppliers in other countries (Able, n.d.).

3.4 Realising Incremental Process and Product Innovation

Incremental process and product innovation have some similar challenges. Notably, existing businesses will often have to develop new processes in order to change their products. However, these types of innovation also face some distinct challenges.

Process innovation can take place completely within an enterprise and can be independent of product decisions. From this perspective, individual organisations have high levels of freedom in terms of engaging in process innovation. However, engaging in process innovation can be a difficult process. Even when firms are exposed to some pressures promoting change, they can be resistant to making changes (Silvestre et al., 2020; Alexander, 2021). As discussed in Section 1, maintaining existing technologies can be based on lock-in mechanisms. Relatedly, adopting new processes can involve discomfort, inefficiency, reorganisation, stress, and perceived risks (Cunningham, 2018; Tura, Keränen, & Patala, 2019). Furthermore, successfully enacting an organisational change can require firms to have particular capabilities. Process upgrading can require technological, organisational, exploitational, explorational, and absorptive capabilities (Zahra & George, 2002; Silvestre et al., 2020). Relatedly, process upgrading can be limited by a lack of technical knowledge and financial resources (Khattak, Stringer, & Benson-Rea, 2015). With all of these factors to consider, process upgrading may not be likely for many small or less well-resourced firms. These dynamics can also apply to the adoption of new processes that are necessary in the implementation of a product innovation.

Incremental process or product innovation can also involve new ventures which may be established to commercialise a new innovation. In such cases, the new ventures are developed to create the new product or implement the new process from the start. This method of introducing an innovation can avoid some of the challenges of undergoing an organisational change.

Service innovation can be very diverse, with each type of service having unique challenges related to its development and implementation. This can include complex technologies such as DNA tracing of cotton as well as low-tech services, such as interviewing garment workers to assess the quality of a factory's management. For many sustainability-focussed services, a key challenge is being able to find customers, which may be fashion brands, producers in garment value chains, or other actors connected to garment value chains.

4 Radical Innovation: Recreating Value Chain and Market Structures

While Section 3 focussed on incremental innovations that can operate within current value chain structures, innovation can also involve more radical changes and result in creating changes to value chain structures. These changes can be small, such as shifting activities between the same sets of actors. They can also be large, such as creating new types of business models, which function completely outside of the existing value chain model. While such activities have more potential for impact, they may face stronger pushback from the dominant socio-technical regime.

This section presents examples of different types of radical innovations that are being developed across the garment industry. Some of these developments can be seen to be incorporating methods connected to the Fourth Industrial Revolution (Schwab, 2016; Schwab & Davis, 2018). This revolution involves technological and organisational developments, which include increased digitisation and new models of connecting production and consumption. Some of the initiatives discussed in the section are in the very early stages and others have achieved some level of scaling. The initiatives discussed include radical production process and product innovation, collaborative production models, new ways of interacting with customers, circular production processes, and mission-oriented endeavours. The section concludes with a consideration of prospects for these types of initiatives to scale.

4.1 Radical Production Process and Product Innovation

Radical product innovation can require radically different production processes or may rely on conventional manufacturing processes. Likewise, radical process innovation can be used to make conventional products as well as new or changed products. Examples of radical production process and product innovation are considered in what follows.

4.1.1 Radical Production Process Innovation

In terms of production processes, research groups and companies are experimenting with new ways to make textiles and garments. Some of these are highly technical. For example, Bolt Threads, a US-based firm, has developed Microsilk, a synthetic version of spider silk which can be knitted or woven into apparel (McDonald, 2018). They have also developed Mylo, in collaboration with another US-based firm called Ecovative, which is a synthetic leather made from mycelium, an element of mushrooms. Both of these techniques create a new product as a result of the new process.

Other forms of process innovation are related to the way that factories are run. Some companies have been experimenting with increasingly automated factories. The fact that garments are typically made with soft materials and often have quickly changing styles has led many to conclude that automation will not be commercially or technically viable. However, some innovators are starting to challenge these assumptions. A recent development related to automating production was the creation of Saitex International's semi-automated jeans factory based in California (Roberts-Islam, 2021). This factory uses far fewer workers than a conventional factory and can quickly ship orders of any size (as little as one piece and up to thousands) to US-based customers.

Another radically new process is 3D knitwear, which involves a knitting machine making an entire garment in one piece. For example, Kniterate is a US-based company that produces 3D knitting machines that can be used for small-scale production (Kniterate, 2022). This technology produces items that are distinctly different from clothing that has been made through conventional processes. These techniques have the benefit of potentially being zero-waste. Items can be made to order and material is not wasted by cutting a pattern out of a larger piece of fabric. They can also have other benefits such as being based on body scans so that they can achieve a perfect fit.

Furthermore, other elements of clothing, such as buttons and embellishments, can be produced through 3D printing processes. Typically, 3D printing is used for creating hard items, such as those made from metal or plastic. For factories manufacturing clothes, this technology creates the potential of being able to produce component parts on-site. Additionally, factories in any part of the value chain could also be able to print spare parts for their machines.

The possibility of developing automated garment production does not have clear-cut implications when it comes to sustainability. An area where the implications are ambiguous is related to jobs. As conventional garment production is based on high levels of human labour, most production takes place in countries with low wage levels. A benefit of this system is that it provides many jobs, often in countries which currently have limited alternative employment options. However, these jobs are often not very high quality. A sustainability challenge that can be created through automation is that jobs may be lost. A counter to this point is that adopting new technology will result in the creation of new types of jobs related to designing, operating, and maintaining new types of equipment.

Automation can also have effects related to environmental impacts. Increased capability for automation can allow production to happen closer to where consumption occurs, which can reduce the need for polluting forms of transportation. Additionally, as mentioned, automated and on-demand production models can reduce the waste generated both during production and through surplus production.

4.1.2 Radical Product Innovation

Many developments are also taking place in relation to product innovation. Some firms are rethinking the nature of garments. One area of development is the creation of electronically enhanced clothing. E-textiles involve electronic devices that can be used for sensing, actuation, communication, and decision-making (Ismar et al., 2020). These products can provide a range of services, which include energy storage, energy harvesting, biosensor applications, sweat sensors, health-care systems, and sports and entertainment technologies. Additionally, smart clothing can also provide a variety of services. AiQ Smart Clothing is a Taiwanese company that is a leader in the smart clothing industry. It produces a variety of products that it describes as having uses in sports coaching, physiotherapy, entertainment, and industry (AiQ Smart Clothing, n.d.).

Developing new functions for garments can address a variety of sustainability challenges. Nevertheless, these developments do also have the potential to create new challenges. One area of risk is that many of these products collect data on wearers, which can lead to concerns related to data ownership and privacy

4.2 Collaborative and Cooperative Production

A variety of actors have been developing collaborative and cooperative business models. Some of these have existed for long periods of time and others have emerged recently. In some cases, these initiatives can connect into more traditional value chain models, such as supplier cooperatives selling to conventional lead firms. Other cooperative forms can represent larger breaks with conventional value chain models.

4.2.1 Cooperatives

One form of collective action that can address sustainability challenges is creating producer cooperatives. A cooperative is defined as 'an autonomous association of persons united voluntarily to meet their common economic, social, and cultural needs and aspirations through a jointly-owned and democratically-controlled enterprise' (International Cooperative Alliance, 2015). Cooperatives can take multiple forms. An organisation that involves a cooperative model promoting sustainable fashion is Yabal Guatemala (Doherty et al., 2020). It is an NGO that works with women's cooperatives that produce items using traditional weaving techniques. The NGO helps to sell the products in local and international markets with the producers receiving fair wages. Yabal uses surplus proceeds and additional donations to provide social programmes for the cooperatives' members.

4.2.2 Industrial Ecosystems

Industrial ecosystems represent another form of collaboration among suppliers. In such systems, a group of businesses, located in close proximity, use each other's waste products as inputs. These collaborative business models have the potential to facilitate zero-waste production. An example of the development of an industrial ecosystem involving garment value chains can be found in the Banwol-Sihwa textiles dyeing cluster in South Korea (Yoon & Nadvi, 2018). As a highly polluting industry, textile dyeing and printing mills felt pressure from national and international regulations, buyers' requirements, and complaints from nearby communities. To respond to these pressures, they first invested in a common effluent treatment plant. Subsequently, they developed an eco-industrial park, which facilitates the exchange of by-products and involves material exchanges with the energy sector and the cement manufacturing sector.

4.3 Servitisation

Another type of business model which can challenge the systems involved in conventional value chains is the growth of servitisation. This phenomenon involves companies leasing products that have conventionally been purchased. Waste can be reduced through this model as multiple people can have access to the services that one product provides. Growth of this type of business model has the potential to radically change how economies function. Potential benefits include better customisation, recurring revenues, deeper customer relationships, a better quality of services provided by products, creating seamless experiences, and cost efficiency and predictability (Aubertin, 2019). Additionally, environmental benefits can be harnessed. Key factors are that this model increases producers' motivation to be efficient and decreases the motivation that conventional manufacturing companies may have to design planned obsolescence into their products. Companies using their product to provide a service have an incentive to make sure it will last as long as possible.

4.3.1 Business-to-Business Models

The servitisation model can be used when businesses produce industrial inputs. Innovation is quite diverse in this area and ranges from IT services to chemical leasing. Consuming industrial inputs as services can result in creating less waste. For example, chemical leasing systems use chemicals more efficiently (UNIDO, 2020). The relationship between user and supplier is restructured, so that instead of users paying for a set amount of a chemical, the user pays for their performance.

A chemical leasing system has been effectively applied by Fabricato S. A., a Colombian textile company (UNIDO, 2020). To carry out sizing (applying a protective coating to yarn during textile production), they were using diverse chemicals, which were creating high levels of pollution through the creation of a high wastewater load involving organic substances. When they introduced a chemical leasing model, which involved payments based on length of fabric treated, they improved the productivity of their processes, increasing the efficiency of raw material use. Overall, chemical consumption was reduced by 30 per cent. This change provided multiple benefits, which included reducing costs, the amount of chemicals sent to the wastewater plant, biological oxygen demand (BOD) (by 99 per cent), chemical oxygen demand (COD) (by 40 per cent), consumption of water (due to reduced cleaning frequency), and dust emissions (improving workers' health and safety).

4.3.2 Business-to Consumer Models

The concept of offering products as services has also been attempted by companies that operate business-to-consumer models. A variety of clothing leasing companies have been developing. For example, the Dutch company

Circos leases baby clothing. These companies can help to reduce frequent purchasing and disposal. However, they can face challenges with consumer acceptance of the idea of wearing garments that have been worn by others.

4.4 Circular Models

New business models are also being created that seek to use circular models. Entrepreneurs have been creative in designing business models, products, and production systems that incorporate circular concepts. In some cases they use simple technology and in other cases these businesses are using cutting-edge technology. Notably, textile recycling can involve both manual and chemical processes, with chemical processes expanding significantly since the year 2000 (Circle Economy, 2020).

One type of emerging business model is for companies to use materials that were previously considered as waste as the inputs for creating new products. In some cases, these are low-tech recycling or reusing initiatives. For example, waste pickers in Senegal collect plastic from landfill sites that is cut into strips to be woven into mats (Maclean, 2022).

Additionally, there are diverse examples of researchers developing new technology that can help with breaking down or reusing items that are currently seen as waste products. In some cases, these can become new types of inputs for creating garments. For example, Lenzing, an Austrian company, produces Rebriba, a textile made from pre- and post-consumer waste cotton. Another example is the Italian company Officina+39 that turns textile waste into a textile dye called Recycrom.

A wide variety of initiatives are taking general waste products and turning them into textiles. These initiatives can involve completely different value chain structures than existing models. Turning post-use garments into inputs for new production requires completely changing relationships in the value chain. Additionally, such models can exclude producers of new raw materials that currently supply garment value chains.

4.5 Social Enterprises

Finally, another type of radical innovation is the creation of businesses which are founded with the purpose of achieving social and environmental objectives. The causes they focus on can be directly related to conditions in value chains, such as hiring people from a disadvantaged group. Alternately, the cause can be tangential to production, such as funding primary schools in areas where production takes place, or completely unrelated, such as giving a portion of proceeds to a selected charity.

Ellilta is a business with a mission. Ellilta is an Ethiopian social enterprise that was founded to provide opportunities for women at risk of sexual exploitation and trafficking (Doherty et al., 2020). It is a private company that is owned by the charity Ellilta Women at Risk (EWR). The business produces scarves and jewellery, with trading profits going to support EWR. Ellilta employs forty-six female artisans, most of whom are former sex workers.

A key form of sustainability innovation in this category is mission-driven businesses focussing on promoting fair trade (Doherty et al., 2020). For example, People Tree is a UK-based fashion brand that was founded in 1991 with a mission to have high ethical and environmental standards in their production processes. The company works with fifty Fairtrade certified producer groups across six countries (Fairtrade, 2022).

Additionally, initiatives tied to causes can take place as intrapreneurship ventures and involve an existing company developing a new product or service with a social or environmental mission. The On Purpose line by Kate Spade, a USA-based fashion house, is an example of this type of initiative (Hope, 2017). Products for this line are created by women in Masoro, a small village in Rwanda. Kate Spade helped set up a factory, which is owned by the Abahizi Dushyigikirane Corporation. The fashion house reports that workers receive wages that are higher than average for the private sector in Rwanda and that they offer a life skills programme that includes access to counselling, information on health, and English lessons.

4.6 Realising Value Chain Structure Innovation

The types of innovation discussed in this section can involve the creation of new business models and changes in the structures of value chains. Some of the potential changes can result in a stronger role for existing lead firms, notably technologies that can facilitate production reshoring, which could include reintegration of manufacturing processes into lead firms and reduce opportunities for specialised producers. Other types of change can involve replacing the current system which is based on large lead firms with, for example, the growth of smaller-scale companies with strong connections to local communities.

While a lot of opportunities exist related to creating new business models, entrepreneurs wishing to develop businesses in new formats can face many challenges. A key challenge is the strong pressures that can exist due to regime pressures pushing for stability in the production system as well as other lock-in mechanisms which favour existing systems. The more radical innovations discussed in this section may face more difficulty being accepted than the incremental innovations discussed in Section 3. However, in some cases, radical product innovations can be incorporated into existing value chain structures, such as a lead firm deciding to include a new type of component part in its supply chain. If this is possible, changes may face fewer barriers than other forms of radical innovation.

Another area of concern is that while new business model ideas may be designed to address a sustainability challenge in a creative way, the ideas need to function as viable businesses as well. This is a challenge which prevents the success of some ventures. Radically new products and processes can face the challenge that they need to find customers who are willing to use them. These customers can be businesses or end users. In some cases, innovations can develop niche markets that can coexist within larger conventional markets. Often business model innovators need to create new markets for their products. This can require firms to have and use dynamic capabilities, which have been defined as the 'ability to integrate, build, and reconfigure internal and external resources/competences to address and shape rapidly changing business environments' (Teece, 2010, p. 692). These capabilities involve firms' capacities to orchestrate activities and resources. Firms may require the ability to create or shape markets in ways that enable them to create and capture value, which can require extending, modifying, or completely revamping their activities to maintain a good fit with their ecosystem or to change their ecosystem. Firms may need to be creative and have strong managerial capacity in order to successfully establish their venture.

Entrepreneurs developing new businesses can face the challenge of being able to compete, especially at the start-up stage. This is particularly the case when an industry has strong incumbents. Overall, business model innovators can benefit from having access to grants or loans that are given with a high risk tolerance, which can support their early-stage development, with both private and public sources of funding playing important roles (Hausmann, Rodrik, & Sabel, 2008). To support the success of radical innovations, governance systems can also be changed in ways that change market dynamics.

A further challenge that can be faced by business model innovators is that some initiatives are not designed in a way which is scalable. Some projects are successful but they rely on systems that only function at a small scale. For example, this can be the case for ventures that rely on artisanal production or the local collection and reuse of waste products.

Despite all of these challenges, many radical innovations are being developed. Some of these initiatives may find ways to break through, especially as the industry is experiencing strong drivers pushing towards the development and adoption of sustainability innovation.

5 Towards a More Sustainable Global Garment Industry

In this Element, we set out to provide students, academics, and practitioners with a comprehensive introduction to the topic of sustainable value chain innovation in the global garment industry. The innovations we have considered cover a variety of economic, social and environmental issues. We have considered instances of the emergence of new ventures as well as intrapreneurship. In addition, we have also considered examples of governance innovation, involving initiatives through which actors seek to shape industry practices. In short, the Element sought answers to five interrelated research questions, which are each explicitly considered in this section.

5.1 What Is Sustainable Value Chain Innovation?

In Section 1, we presented a definition of sustainability that is based on economic, social, and environmental pillars. We also identified key features of value chains. Typical garment industry value chains were shown to have highly fragmented structures, which can involve a strong role of lead firms. Innovation was described as involving learning and engaging in new practices. While diverse innovations, whether small or large, emerge on a regular basis, the ability for these innovations to scale and have large levels of impact is often limited by stability reinforced through the structures of socio-technical landscapes and socio-technical regimes. Furthermore, we also identified that sustainable value chain innovation can involve direct industrial innovation or governance innovation that is focussed on changing other actors' behaviours.

5.2 What Are the Key Drivers behind This Kind of Innovation?

We have identified multiple drivers leading to increased international interest in sustainable value chain innovation in the global garment industry. One key driver is the prevalence of sustainability challenges connected to the garment industry. A critical element is the global climate crisis. Additionally, it has become increasingly apparent that the fast-fashion model dominating the industry leads to unsustainable production and consumption patterns, as well as environmental and social downgrading pressures.

A second driver is the creation of campaigns and policies designed to encourage value chain actors to address sustainability challenges. Notably, the demands of the Paris Agreement on climate change have prompted a need within the global garment industry to contribute towards the overall objective of broad-based decarbonisation. Furthermore, multiple other new legislative developments have prompted the need for sustainable value chain innovation. Notably, several countries have enacted legislation that seeks to combat modern slavery, increase value chain transparency, require human rights and environmental due diligence, and promote sustainable production and a circular economy.

A third driver is identified as a growing market demand for products and services that claim to be more sustainable. This demand can come from customers as well as employees. Businesses may feel strong incentives to make changes due to this demand. However, acting based on this motivation may heighten the potential that implemented innovations may solely be branded as a way to address a sustainability issue, without actually involving impactful changes.

Finally, in this Element we suggested that sustainable value chain innovation is also driven by a number of interrelated value chain disruptions and increased volatility in global markets that are prompting brands, retailers, and producers to search for new and innovative ways of overcoming such risks associated with value chain participation. Experiencing these diverse disruptions has increased the need for risk management within the garment industry, including the need to find new ways of ensuring the economic, social, and environmental sustainability of GVCs.

However, while these four factors can drive sustainability action, the necessary tools, knowledge, insights, and expertise do not always exist to adequately respond to these pressures. A strong need has thus been created for the invention of new products, production processes, organisational structures, technological solutions, and documentation formats that can respond to emerging demands. For example, there is a distinct knowledge gap in relation to how the global garment industry should decarbonise.

5.3 Who Are the Actors Involved in Sustainable Value Chain Innovation?

In this Element, we identify a diverse range of actors that have been engaging in sustainable value chain innovation in the garment industry. These actors include existing businesses, which can range from microenterprises to large multinational corporations. Innovation can also involve new start-ups. Additionally, public sectors actors have also been shown to be involved in innovative activities. Finally, a broad set of social actors, such as NGOs, are also involved in sustainable value chain innovation. All of these actors can engage in direct industrial innovation or governance innovation intended to change the behaviour of other actors.

5.4 Which Innovative Practices Do These Actors Claim to Engage In?

In Section 2, we mapped out a range of governance innovations. As a key part of value chain governance is the strong roles played by lead firms, this section explored how these actors use their power to organise and initiate sustainability innovation in GVCs. Moreover, we argued that governmental actors at multiple scales play an important role in terms of shaping the institutional contexts in which sustainable value chain innovation takes place. The section also identified producers, unions, workers, NGOs, support service providers, media, and educators as governance actors in sustainable value chain innovation.

Sections 3 and 4 sought to map out actors' involvement in industrial aspects of sustainable value chain innovation. Here, we made a distinction between incremental and radical innovative practices in GVCs. To begin with, Section 3 laid out examples of incremental process and product innovation. The section considered firm-level process innovation, physical product innovation, and a wide variety of service innovations. The service innovations covered included conventional production and trade-related services, as well as new sustainability-focussed services, such as those related to sustainability standards and auditing, traceability, capacity-building support, consulting, and consumer communication.

Section 4 moved on to scrutinise what we consider to be more radical forms of sustainability innovation. These innovations often seek to recreate value chain and market structures. The section presented examples of radical product and production process innovation, collaborative and cooperative forms of production (such as cooperatives and industrial ecosystems), servitisation (including business-to-business models and business-to-consumer models), circular models, and social enterprise models.

A critical contribution of this Element has thus been to document, analyse, and categorise various forms of garment industry sustainable value chain innovation that diverse actors claim to be undertaking. However, in this Element, we have not undertaken any systematic assessments that can validate (or discredit) the sustainability claims made by innovators. Nonetheless, given the plethora of initiatives and diversity of creators, it is likely that at least some of these initiatives do have the potential to achieve their stated objectives.

5.5 Why Are These Practices Likely to Be (Un)successful in Achieving Their Aims?

Regardless of the specific technologies and programme designs involved in any particular innovation, a key issue is that they are emerging within the existing industry conditions. Here, we highlight some of the main lessons learned and theoretical insights from earlier GVC and sustainability literatures which should allow us to, at least in theory, assess the extent to which sustainable value chain innovation can contribute towards a broader industry transformation.

One useful entry point into this discussion may be to highlight what sustainable value chain innovation cannot do. At one level, what counts as a 'sustainable' value chain is in itself highly disputed. There are widely different perceptions among value chain actors of what constitutes 'sustainable' forms of production, consumption, transportation, and marketing of products/services (Riisgaard et al., 2020; Krauss & Krishnan, 2022). For instance, by what criteria do we assess whether one form of cotton production is more sustainable than another approach to cotton production? Are organic, fairtrade, or Better Cotton more sustainable approaches to cotton production and trading? According to recent research, this really depends upon whether observers, or value chain actors for that matter, place greater emphasis on increasing farmer earnings and worker wages, reducing environmental pollution, or, for instance, eradicating child labour from cotton production in the Global South (Ghori et al., 2022). These economic, social, and environmental objectives which are related to (often) innovative, new ways of growing cotton are sometimes contradictory (Lund-Thomsen et al., 2021). For instance, reducing the need for spraying cotton plants with pesticides may reduce the risk of cotton workers being exposed to pesticide poisoning. However, if the spraying of pesticides is reduced or no longer required (e.g., in organic cotton production), this may also reduce the amount of work available and thus the income of farm workers (Ghori et al., 2022).

Adding to this complexity is the fact that even if it is possible to verify that one form of cotton production is more sustainable than another, the implementation of sustainability standards may be highly uneven and their positive or negative impacts depend upon factors such as different climatic conditions, plagues and pests, existing capabilities of agricultural producers, enabling legislation, and the varying technical and implementation expertise of implementing partners of sustainability standard systems (Ghori et al., 2022). Hence, the implementation of the same standard may yield widely different economic, social, and environmental outcomes for farmers and farm workers across different geographical contexts and time periods, making it virtually impossible to assess the more 'generic' sustainability effects associated with innovative forms of sustainable value chain innovation, such as the introduction of new sustainability standards (Bartley, 2018; Van der Ven & Cashore, 2018).

While we have highlighted the potential of value chain innovation to contribute to broader sustainability objectives, it is also important to highlight that many forms of (incremental) innovation do not fundamentally challenge the structure of what we refer to as 'the political ecology of global pollution outsourcing' in the garment and textile industries. From a political ecology perspective, governance of GVCs can be seen as lead firms attempting to exert control over the environment of others by influencing the location of the sites at which industrial pollution is generated and released into the environment (Bryant & Bailey, 1997). Power here is associated with minimising the costs associated with the production process. From a GVC perspective, this means trying to actively manage the tensions between cost minimisation, profit maximisation, and externalising the economic, social, and environmental risks associated with the production of goods and services (Ponte, 2019, 2020). For instance, the outsourcing of garment and textile production could be seen as related to cost-cutting by geographically redistributing fire and building safety risks, costs of employment (increasing the risk of forced and child labour), and pollution burdens to cheaper producer countries, where local workers and communities face increased exposure to occupational and safety risks as well as hazardous environmental pollution (Bick et al., 2018; Lund-Thomsen, 2022).

This line of reasoning also finds support in recent work on ecologically unequal exchange and uneven development patterns along GVCs. Thus, Althouse et al. (2021) argue that the ecologically unequal exchange literature has empirically demonstrated how material and energy resources are transferred from low-income to high-income countries. In theoretical terms, the authors suggest that unequal ecological exchange can be traced to developing country participation in GVCs. They suggest that countries can fall into three groupings based on social, ecological, productive, and GVC patterns. They name the first the 'curse of GVC marginalisation' in which countries at the margins of GVCs experience poor economic and social outcomes as well as ecological degradation. They label the second 'ecologically perverse upgrading', which involves country integration into GVCs with beneficial productive and socio-economic outcomes that are obtained at the cost of higher-than-average local ecological degradation. Finally, Althouse and coauthors' third category is 'reproduction of the core', which is made up of countries that reap most of the benefits from GVC participation, due to high levels of value-capture and high incomes, while being exposed to lower levels of environmental degradation/pollution. While the notion of unequal ecological exchange involves a slightly different emphasis than the 'political ecology of global outsourcing' concept, both notions imply that some forms of value chain innovation will contribute little more than marginal steps towards a fundamental sustainability transition within the garment and textile industries. Both notions highlight that sustainable value chain innovation takes place within this broader context of global pollution outsourcing/unequal ecological exchange.

The way innovation will proceed in addressing sustainability challenges connected to the garment industry is yet to be determined. As noted in Section 1, radical innovation can be the product of multiple incremental innovations. The nature of how technological developments scale can be shaped by how users adopt them, the policy environment, cultural discourse, infrastructure systems, and maintenance networks in which they operate (Geels, 2002).

The wide number of existing and soon-to-emerge innovations related to garment industry sustainability have the potential to address a diverse range of complex sustainability challenges. A positive outcome could be that this diversity can lead to the breakthrough of the most viable practices which help to address critical sustainability challenges. However, sustainable value chain innovation is not a panacea. The realisation of a movement towards the adoption of sustainable systems faces a number of challenges.

(1) *Trends and current events may shape behaviour more than urgency of sustainability challenges.* Large lead firms often rapidly change the focus of their actions to address ever-changing emerging hot topics. Actions lack coordination related to the priority or strategic ordering of implementation processes.

(2) *Success can be based on market viability as opposed to the ability to address sustainability challenges.* A great diversity of initiatives are being developed which may have differing levels of impact on sustainability challenges. However, those that have the most success (or scale) may be the ones with higher market appeal, which can be disconnected from sustainability-related impacts.

(3) *New systems may put increased pressure on producers in developing countries.* Suppliers being asked to comply with an increasing volume of standards may create downward pressure on local sustainability-related conditions, such as wages.

(4) *Experimentation is often driven by individuals' perspectives rather than a systemic evaluation of situations.* Some challenges may be ignored by entrepreneurs as the sustainability issues they focus on may reflect their awareness of challenges as opposed to the most pressing challenges.

(5) *Existing markets can absorb change as opposed to innovation leading to systemic change.* Sustainable ventures are often limited to operating within existing markets (or within existing large businesses) while most businesses continue to use practices associated with sustainability challenges. Furthermore, this dynamic can lead to radical innovations failing because they cannot fit into existing systems.

As demonstrated throughout this Element, innovators around the world have been developing an extensive number of initiatives that seek to address sustainability challenges and achieve sustainability-related goals. Overall, sustainable value chain innovation is a way for diverse actors to help generate solutions to current and emerging sustainability challenges at different scales. Yet the theorisation of these initiatives and empirical investigations of their effectiveness are only still in a very nascent stage and remain key areas for further investigation and analysis in the years to come. Learning from ongoing actions and experimentation across a broad set of opportunities and challenges may help to support the development of more impactful initiatives in the future.

5.6 Implications

The dynamics discussed in this Element can provide guidance for future research on sustainable value chain innovation. Notwithstanding the above caveats, a number of questions can be asked and multiple areas can be explored further to develop a deeper understanding of sustainable value chain innovation. Future explorations can take diverse approaches. For instance, research can focus on the perspective of a particular value chain actor, such as a firm (e.g., a retailer or producer), and consider how they are embedded in existing systems and the potential they have to engage in innovation for sustainability versus their incentives to maintain the current system. Alternatively, research can focus on a specific product, either a conventional one or one based on a new sustainability innovation, and explore the systems involved in its creation and its potential after-use outcomes. In a similar vein, studies can focus on a particular governance innovation and explore the dynamics involved (e.g., identifying key actors and considering how its pressures or incentives are felt by different stakeholder groups). Key issues to consider also include broader implications of changes to the geography of production (Gong et al., 2022). For example, how would increasing levels of local production impact countries that rely on garment exports? Research on innovation for sustainability can also focus on specific production sites, such as industrial clusters or eco-parks. Such studies can explore relationships within the site and how the site connects to GVCs. Finally, research can also focus on a particular sustainability challenge facing the garment industry, identify options which are available for creating alternative systems, and consider barriers or opportunities for these options to be successful. Critical issues to explore in a study on innovation for sustainability include the dynamics of landscape and regime pressures.

Additionally, the issues discussed in this Element have implications for policy and practice. As shown throughout, sustainable value chain innovation within the garment industry involves diverse global initiatives. All of the actors involved work within a landscape that includes socio-technical regimes that promote stability. However, value chains for consumer goods are experiencing changing landscape conditions. Key ongoing trends include growing global attention on climate change, the growth of middle-class consumers around the world, and expanding technological developments shaping markets, such as the rapid expansion of online purchasing. These emerging trends may create cracks in the stabilising power of existing regimes and more opportunities for sustainability innovations to break through and scale.

References

Able (n.d.). Able is moving fashion forward. [Online]. www.livefashionable
.com/pages/about-able (accessed 28 April 2022).

Accord on Fire and Building Safety in Bangladesh. (n.d.). About. [Online].
https://bangladeshaccord.org/about (accessed 28 April 2022).

AiQ Smart Clothing. (n.d.). Products and services. [Online]. www.aiqs
martclothing.com/product-service (accessed 28 April 2022).

Alexander, R. (2018). Sustainability in global production networks: Introducing the
notion of extended supplier networks. *Competition & Change*, 22(3), 255–73.

Alexander, R. (2020). Emerging roles of lead buyer governance for sustainability
across global production networks. *Journal of Business Ethics*, 162(2), 269–90.

Alexander, R. (2021). Governance in global production networks and local sustainability challenges: Experiences of sustainability transitions in cotton garment
production in India. In M. B. Rana & M. M. C. Allen, eds., *Upgrading the
Global Garment Industry*. Cheltenham: Edward Elgar Publishing, pp. 339–61.

Alexander, R. (2022). Limits of buyer-driven governance for sustainability:
Inherent challenges of fragmented supplier networks. *Journal of Economic
Geography*, 22(4), 801–28.

Alexander, R. & Lund-Thomsen, P. (2021). *Sustainable Value Chain
Entrepreneurship: A Guidebook*. Copenhagen: Center for Business and
Development Studies, Copenhagen Business School.

Alford, M., Barrientos, S., & Visser, M. (2017). Multi-scalar labour agency in
global production networks: Contestation and crisis in the South African fruit
sector. *Development and Change*, 48(4), 721–45.

Althouse, J., Schichowski, B. C., Cahen-Fourot, L., Duran, C., & Knauss, S.
(2021). Ecological uneven exchange and uneven development patterns along
global value chains. Vienna Institute for Ecological Economics Working
Paper No. 42/2021. https://epub.wu-wien.ac.at/8529/1/WP_42.pdf (accessed
28 April 2022).

Amfori. (n.d.). About Amfori. [Online]. www.amfori.org/content/about-amfori
(accessed 28 April 2022).

Anner, M. (2015). Labor control regimes and worker resistance in global supply
chains. *Labor History*, 56(3), 292–307.

Anner, M. (2018). CSR participation committees, wildcat strikes and the sourcing squeeze in global supply chains. *British Journal of Industrial Relations*,
56(1), 75–98.

Anner, M. (2021). Power relations in global supply chains and the unequal distribution of costs during crises: Squeezing suppliers and workers during the COVID-19 pandemic. *International Labour Review*, 161(1), 59–82.

Ashwin, S., Oka, C., Schüßler, E., Alexander, R., & Lohmeyer, N. (2020). Spillover effects across transnational industrial relations agreements: The potential and limits of collective action in global supply chains. *ILR Review*, 73(4), 995–1020.

Aubertin, C. (2019). From product to product-as-a-service: A new business model shaping the future of industries. *Medium*, 2 July. https://medium.com/swlh/from-product-to-product-as-a-service-37baed471cd6 (accessed 28 April 2022).

Bair, J. (2008). Analysing global economic organization: Embedded networks and global chains compared. *Economy and Society*, 37(3), pp. 339–64.

Barrientos, S., Gereffi, G., & Rossi, A. (2011). Economic and social upgrading in global production networks: A new paradigm for a changing world. *International Labour Review*, 150(3–4), 319–340.

Bartley, T. (2018). *Rules without Rights: Land, Labor, and Private Authority in the Global Economy*. Oxford: Oxford University Press.

Bartley, T. & Child, C. (2011). Movements, markets and fields: The effects of anti-sweatshop campaigns on US firms, 1993–2000. *Social Forces*, 90(2), 425–51.

Bartley, T. & Child, C. (2014). Shaming the corporation: The social production of targets and the anti-sweatshop movement. *American Sociological Review*, 79(4), 653–79.

Berg, A., Magnus, K.-H., Granskog, A. et al. (2020). *Fashion on Climate: How the Fashion Industry Can Urgently Act to Reduce Its Greenhouse-Gas Emissions*. Copenhagen: McKinsey & Global Fashion Agenda.

BGMEA (Bangladesh Garment Manufacturers and Exporters Association). (2021). *BGMEA: Sustainability Report 2020*. Dhaka: BGMEA.

Bick, R., Halsey, E., & Ekenga, C. C. (2018). The global environmental injustice of fast fashion. *Environmental Health*, 17(1), 1–4.

Binz, C. & Truffer, B. (2017). Global innovation systems: A conceptual framework for innovation dynamics in transnational contexts. *Research Policy*, 46 (7), 1284–98.

Blankenship, H., Kulhavy, V., & Lagneryd, J. (2009). Introducing strategic sustainable development in a business incubator. *Progress in Industrial* Ecology: *An International Journal*, 6(3), 243–64.

Boltanski, L. & Thévenot. L. (1991). *De la justification: Les économies de la grandeur*. Paris: Gallimard.

Brooks, A. (2019). *Clothing Poverty: The Hidden World of Fast Fashion and Second-Hand Clothes*. London: Bloomsbury Publishing.

Brown, D. & Knudsen, J. S. (2015). Domestic institutions and market pressures as drivers of corporate social responsibility: Company initiatives in Denmark and the UK. *Political Studies*, 63(1), 181–201.

Bryant, R. L. & Bailey, S. (1997). *Third World Political Ecology*. Hove: Psychology Press.

Carrasco Rozas, A. (2017). Sustainable textile innovations: Coffee ground fibre. *Fashion United*, 16 June. https://fashionunited.uk/news/fashion/sustainable-tex tile-innovations-coffee-ground-fibre/2017061624856 (accessed 28 April 2022).

Carroll, A. B. (1979). A three-dimensional conceptual model of corporate performance. *Academy of Management Review*, 4(4), 497–505.

Choi, T. Y., Dooley, K. J., & Rungtusanatham, M. (2001). Supply networks and complex adaptive systems: Control versus emergence. *Journal of Operations Management*, 19(3), 351–66.

Circle Economy. (2020). *Recycled Post-Consumer Textiles: An Industry Perspective*. Lille: Interreg North-West Europe Fibersort Project. http://bit .ly/3cpkeh3 (accessed 28 April 2022).

Cirino, E. (2018). The environment's new clothes: Biodegradable textiles grown from live organisms. *Scientific American*, 14 September. www.scien tificamerican.com/article/the-environments-new-clothes-biodegradable-tex tiles-grown-from-live-organisms (accessed 28 April 2022).

Coe, N. M., Dicken, P., & Hess, M. (2008). Global production networks: Realizing the potential. *Journal of Economic Geography*, 8(3), 271–95.

Coe, N. M. & Yeung, H. W.-C. (2015). *Global Production Networks: Theorizing Economic Development in an Interconnected World*. Oxford: Oxford University Press.

Cunningham, S. (2018). *Framing the Concepts That Underpin Discontinuous Technological Change, Technology Capability and Absorptive Capacity*. Pretoria: Trade & Industrial Policy Strategies (TIPS). www.tips.org.za/ research-archive/trade-and-industry/item/download/1721_83368b23d40c5113 28ac1f1102b10153 (accessed 28 April 2022).

Dadush, U. (2022). The future of global value chains and the role of the WTO. World Trade Organization (WTO) Staff Working Paper No. ERSD-2022–11. www.wto .org/english/res_e/reser_e/ersd202211_e.pdf (accessed 14 March 2023).

Dallas, M. P., Ponte, S., & Sturgeon, T. J. (2019). Power in global value chains. *Review of International Political Economy*, 26(4), 666–94.

D'Ambrogio, E. (2014). Workers' conditions in the textile and clothing sector: Just an Asian affair? European Parliamentary Research Service Briefing August 2014. www.europarl.europa.eu/EPRS/140841REV1-Workers-condi tions-in-the-textile-and-clothing-sector-just-an-Asian-affair-FINAL.pdf (accessed 28 April 2022).

De Bakker, F. G., Rasche, A., & Ponte, S. (2019). Multi-stakeholder initiatives on sustainability: A cross-disciplinary review and research agenda for business ethics. *Business Ethics Quarterly*, 29(3), 343–83.

De Marchi, V. & Alford, M. (2022). State policies and upgrading in global value chains: A systematic literature review. *Journal of International Business Policy*, 5(1), 88–111.

De Marchi, V., Di Maria, E., Krishnan, A., & Ponte, S. (2019). Environmental upgrading in global value chains. In S. Ponte, G. Gereffi, & G. Raj-Reichert, eds., *Handbook on Global Value Chains*. Cheltenham: Edward Elgar Publishing, pp. 310–23.

De Marchi, V., Giuliani, E., & Rabellotti, R. (2018). Do global value chains offer developing countries learning and innovation opportunities? *The European Journal of Development Research*, 30(3), 389–407.

Doherty, B., Haugh, H., Sahan, E., Wills, T., & Croft, S. (2020). *Creating the New Economy: Business Models That Put People and Planet First.* Culemborg and Gateshead: World Fair Trade Organization and Traidcraft. https://wfto.com/sites/default/files/Business_Models_Report.pdf (accessed 28 April 2022).

Doyle, M. (2021). These 6 traceability technologies could help clean up the fashion industry. *Ecocult*, 29 March. https://ecocult.com/traceability-tech nologies-fashion-supply-chain (accessed 28 April 2022).

Dumitrescu, I., Mocioiu, A. M., & Visileanu, E. (2008). Cleaner production in Romanian textile industry: A case study. *International Journal of Environmental Studies*, 65(4), 549–62.

(E) BrandConnect. (2020). Sustainable style: Fashion supply chains make green gains. [Online]. www.maersk.com/news/articles/2020/12/08/sustainable-style (accessed 28 April 2022).

EU (European Union). (2020). *A New Circular Economy Action Plan: For a Cleaner and More Competitive Europe*. Brussels: European Commission.

EU (European Union). (2022a). Just and sustainable economy: Commission lays down rules for companies to respect human rights and environment in global value chains. European Commission Press Release, 23 February. https://ec.europa.eu/commission/presscorner/detail/en/ip_22_1145 (accessed 28 April 2022).

EU (European Union). (2022b). *Strategy for Sustainable and Circular Textiles*. COM/2022/141. Brussels: European Commission.

EU (European Union). (n.d.). Social enterprises. [Online]. https://ec.europa.eu/growth/sectors/proximity-and-social-economy/social-economy-eu/social-enterprises_en (accessed 28 April 2022).

Euromonitor. (2021). Passport [database]. London: Euromonitor.

Euronext. (2022). Guide to the latest ESG EU regulatory guidelines. [Online] www.euronext.com/en/news/esg-laws-regulation (accessed 24 January 2023).

European Parliament. (2021). Circular economy: Definition, importance and benefits. European Parliament News [Online], 5 December. www.europarl .europa.eu/news/en/headlines/economy/20151201STO05603/circular-econ omy-definition-importance-and-benefits (accessed 28 April 2022).

Fairtrade. (2022). People Tree. [Online]. www.fairtrade.org.uk/buying-fair trade/cotton-draft/people-tree/ (accessed 28 April 2022).

Fecht, S. (2021). How exactly does carbon dioxide cause global warming? *State of the Planet* [Columbia Climate School], 25 February. https://news.climate .columbia.edu/2021/02/25/carbon-dioxide-cause-global-warming (accessed 28 April 2022).

FICCA (Fashion Industry Charter for Climate Action). (2021). *Fashion Industry Charter for Climate Action Progress Report*. Bonn: UN Climate Change. www.fashioncharter.org (accessed 28 April 2022).

Ford, M. & Gillan, M. (2021). Living wage initiatives in the garment sector: Insights from Southeast Asia. In T. Dobbins & P. Prowse, eds., *The Living Wage*. London: Routledge, pp. 191–205.

Fox, T., Ward, H., & Howard, B. (2002). *Public Sector Roles in Strengthening Corporate Social Responsibility*. Washington, DC: World Bank.

Fransen, L. (2013). The embeddedness of responsible business practice: Exploring the interaction between national-institutional environments and corporate social responsibility. *Journal of Business Ethics*, 115(2), 213–27.

Fransen, L., & Burgoon, B. (2014). Privatizing or socializing corporate responsibility: Business participation in voluntary programs. *Business & Society*, 53 (4), 583–619.

Fransen, L., Kolk, A., & Rivera-Santos, M. (2019). The multiplicity of international corporate social responsibility standards. *Multinational Business Review*, 27(4), 397–426.

Fu, X. (2020). Digital transformation of global value chains and sustainable post-pandemic recovery. *Transnational Corporations Journal*, 27(2), 157–66.

Geels, F. W. (2002). Technological transitions as evolutionary reconfiguration processes: A multi-level perspective and a case-study. *Research Policy*, 31 (8–9), 1257–74.

Geels, F. W. (2004). From sectoral systems of innovation to socio-technical systems: Insights about dynamics and change from sociology and institutional theory. *Research Policy*, 33(6–7), 897–920.

Geels, F. W. (2019). Socio-technical transitions to sustainability: A review of criticisms and elaborations of the multi-level perspective. *Current Opinion in Environmental Sustainability*, 39, 187–201.

Geels, F. W. & Kemp, R. (2007). Dynamics in socio-technical systems: Typology of change processes and contrasting case studies. *Technology in Society*, 29(4), 441–55.

Genus, A. & Coles, A. M. (2008). Rethinking the multi-level perspective of technological transitions. *Research Policy*, 37(9), 1436–45.

Gereffi. G. (1994). The organization of buyer-driven global commodity chains: How U.S. retailers shape overseas production networks. In G. Gereffi & M. Korzeniewicz, eds., *Commodity Chains and Global Capitalism*. Westport, CT: Praeger, pp. 95–122.

Gereffi, G. (1999). International trade and industrial upgrading in the apparel commodity chain. *Journal of International Economics*, 48(1), 37–70.

Gereffi, G., Humphrey, J., & Sturgeon, T. (2005). The governance of global value chains. *Review of International Political Economy*, 12(1), 78–104.

Gereffi, G. & Lee, J. (2016). Economic and social upgrading in global value chains and industrial clusters: Why governance matters. *Journal of Business Ethics*, 133(1), 25–38.

Gereffi, G. & Mayer, F. (2006). Globalization and the demand for governance. In G. Gereffi, ed., *The New Offshoring of Jobs and Global Development*. Geneva: International Labour Office (ILO), pp. 39–58.

Gereffi, G., Posthuma, A. C., & Rossi, A. (2021). Introduction: Disruptions in global value chains – continuity or change for labour governance? *International Labour Review*, 160(4), 501–17.

Ghori, S., Lund-Thomsen, P., Gallemore, C., Singh, S., & Riisgaard, L. (2022). Compliance and cooperation in global value chains: The effects of the Better Cotton Initiative in Pakistan and India. *Ecological Economics*, 193, 107312.

Giuliani, E., Pietrobelli, C., & Rabellotti, R. (2005). Upgrading in global value chains: Lessons from Latin American clusters. *World development*, 33(4), 549–573.

Goldenberg, E. (2014). Investing in workers through financial education: HERfinance curriculum launch. [Online]. www.bsr.org/en/our-insights/blog-view/investing-in-workers-through-financial-education-herfinance-curriculum-laun (accessed 28 April 2022).

Gong, H., Hassink, R., Foster, C., Hess, M., & Garretsen, H. (2022). Globalisation in reverse? Reconfiguring the geographies of value chains and production networks. *Cambridge Journal of Regions, Economy and Society*, 15(2), 165–181.

Hausmann, R., Rodrik, D., & Sabel, C. (2008). Reconfiguring industrial policy: A framework with an application to South Africa. Harvard University Center for International Development Working Paper No. 168/Harvard Kennedy

School Faculty Research Working Paper No. RWP08-031. https://growthlab
.cid.harvard.edu/files/growthlab/files/2008-5-cid-working-paper-168-south-
africa-industrial-policy.pdf (accessed 28 April 2022).

Hekkert, M. P., Suurs, R. A., Negro, S. O., Kuhlmann, S., & Smits, R. E.
(2007). Functions of innovation systems: A new approach for analysing
technological change. *Technological Forecasting and Social Change*, 74
(4), 413–32.

Henderson, J., Dicken, P., Hess, M., Coe, N., & Yeung, H. W. C. (2002). Global
production networks and the analysis of economic development. *Review of
International Political Economy*, 9(3), 436–64.

Henninger, C. E., Alevizou, P. J., Goworek, H., & Ryding, D. (2017). *Sustainability
in Fashion: A Cradle to Upcycle Approach*. Cham: Palgrave Macmillan.

Hess, M. (2004). 'Spatial' relationships? Towards a reconceptualization of
embeddedness. *Progress in Human Geography*, 28(2), 165–86.

Hope, K. (2017). What makes this Kate Spade bag unusual? *BBC News*, 26 July.
www.bbc.com/news/business-40682888 (accessed 28 April 2022).

Hopkins, T. & Wallerstein, I. (1977). Patterns of Development of the Modern
World-System. *Review*, 1(2), 11-145.

Horner, R. & Nadvi, K. (2018). Global value chains and the rise of the Global
South: Unpacking twenty-first century polycentric trade. *Global Networks*,
18(2), 207–37.

Humphrey, J. & Schmitz, H. (2002). How does insertion in global value chains
affect upgrading in industrial clusters? *Regional Studies*, 36(9), 1017–27.

Idowu, S. O. & Schmidpeter R. (2015). Corporate social responsibility in
Europe: An Introduction. In S. O. Idowu, R. Schmidpeter, & M. S. Fifka,
eds., *Corporate Social Responsibility in Europe: United in Sustainable
Diversity*. Cham: Springer, pp. 1–16.

International Cooperative Alliance. (2015). *Guidance Notes to the Co-operative
Principles*. Brussels: International Cooperative Alliance. www.ica.coop/
sites/default/files/2021-11/ICA%20Guidance%20Notes%20EN.pdf
(accessed 28 April 2022).

Ismar, E., Kurşun Bahadir, S., Kalaoglu, F., & Koncar, V. (2020). Futuristic
clothes: Electronic textiles and wearable technologies. *Global Challenges*, 4
(7), 1900092.

Jackson, G. & Apostolakou, A. (2010). Corporate social responsibility in
Western Europe: An institutional mirror or substitute? *Journal of Business
Ethics*, 94(3), 371–94.

Jensen, F. & Whitfield, L. (2022). Leveraging participation in global apparel
supply chains through green industrialization strategies: Implications for
low-income countries. *Ecological Economics*, 194, 107331.

Jurowetzki, R., Lema, R., & Lundvall, B. Å. (2018). Combining innovation systems and global value chains for development: Towards a research agenda. *The European Journal of Development Research*, 30(3), 364–88.

Kaplinsky, R. & Morris, M. (2002). *A Handbook for Value Chain Research.* www.fao.org/fileadmin/user_upload/fisheries/docs/Value_Chain_Handbool .pdf (accessed 28 April 2022).

Kemp, R., Loorbach, D., & Rotmans, J. (2007). Transition management as a model for managing processes of co-evolution towards sustainable development. *The International Journal of Sustainable Development & World Ecology*, 14(1), 78–91.

Kern, F., Rogge, K. S., & Howlett, M. (2019). Policy mixes for sustainability transitions: New approaches and insights through bridging innovation and policy studies. *Research Policy*, 48(10), 103832.

Khan, M. J., Ponte, S., & Lund-Thomsen, P. (2020). The 'factory manager dilemma': Purchasing practices and environmental upgrading in apparel global value chains. *Environment and Planning A*, 52(4), 766–89.

Khattak, A., Stringer, C., Benson-Rea, M., & Haworth, N. (2015). Environmental upgrading of apparel firms in global value chains: Evidence from Sri Lanka. *Competition & Change*, 19(4), 317–35.

Kleibert, J. M. (2016). Pervasive but neglected: Conceptualising services and global production networks. *Geography Compass*, 10(8), 333–45.

Klein, N. (2000). *No Logo: Taking Aim at the Brand Bullies.* London: Picador.

Klitkou, A., Bolwig, S., Hansen, T., & Wessberg, N. (2015). The role of lock-in mechanisms in transition processes: The case of energy for road transport. *Environmental Innovation and Societal Transitions*, 16, 22–37.

Kniterate. (2022). About us. [Online]. www.kniterate.com/about (accessed 28 April 2022).

Knudsen, J. S., Moon, J., & Slager, R. (2015). Government policies for corporate social responsibility in Europe: A comparative analysis of institutionalisation. *Policy & Politics*, 43(1), 81–99.

Krauss, J. (2017). What is cocoa sustainability? Mapping stakeholders' socio-economic, environmental, and commercial constellations of priorities. *Enterprise Development & Microfinance*, 28(3), 228–50.

Krauss, J. E. & Krishnan, A. (2022). Global decisions versus local realities: Sustainability standards, priorities and upgrading dynamics in agricultural global production networks. *Global Networks*, 22(1), 65–88.

Kumar, R. (2017). Prospects of sustainable fashion innovation. *International Journal of Textile and Fashion Technology*, 7(6), 5–14.

Kwon, H., Bae, J., Lee, J., & Chung, S.W. (2021). Toward a bipolar apparel GVC? From the perspective of first-tier suppliers. *Journal of Asian Sociology*, 50(1), 9–32.

Langford, N. J. (2019). The governance of social standards in emerging markets: An exploration of actors and interests shaping Trustea as a Southern multi-stakeholder initiative. *Geoforum*, 104, 81–91.

Langford, N. J., Nadvi, K., & Braun-Munzinger, C. (2022). The shaping of 'Southern' sustainability standards in a value chain world: Comparative evidence from China and India. *Review of International Political Economy*. doi.org/10.1080/09692290.2022.2089713.

LeBaron, G. & Rühmkorf, A. (2017). Steering CSR through home state regulation: A comparison of the impact of the UK Bribery Act and Modern Slavery Act on global supply chain governance. *Global Policy*, 8(S3), 15–28.

Lema, R., Pietrobelli, C., & Rabellotti, R. (2019). Innovation in global value chains. In S. Ponte, G. Gereffi, & G. Raj-Reichert, eds., *Handbook on Global Value Chains*. Cheltenham: Edward Elgar Publishing, pp. 370–84.

Lema, R., Rabellotti, R., & Gehl Sampath, P. (2018). Innovation trajectories in developing countries: Co-evolution of global value chains and innovation systems. *The European Journal of Development Research*, 30(3), 345–63.

Levi Strauss. (2010). It's time to ban sandblasting. [Online.] www.levistrauss.com/2010/09/07/its-time-ban-sandblasting/ (accessed 24 January 2023).

Levy, D. L. (2008). Political contestation in global production networks. *Academy of Management Review*, 33(4), 943–63.

Li, C. (2021). From insurgency to movement: An embryonic labor movement undermining hegemony in south China. *ILR Review*, 74(4), 843–74.

Locke, R. M. (2013). *The Promise and Limits of Private Power: Promoting Labor Standards in a Global Economy*. Cambridge: Cambridge University Press.

Locke, R. M., Amengual, M., & Mangla, A. (2009). Virtue out of necessity? Compliance, commitment, and the improvement of labor conditions in global supply chains. *Politics & Society*, 37(3), 319–51.

Loorbach, D., Frantzeskaki, N., & Avelino, F. (2017). Sustainability transitions research: Transforming science and practice for societal change. *Annual Review of Environment and Resources*, 42, 599–626.

Lu, S. (2020). *Fashion Industry Benchmarking Study*. Washington, DC: United States Fashion Industry Association. www.usfashionindustry.com/pdf_files/20210715-fashion-industry-benchmarking-survey.pdf (accessed 28 April 2022).

Lukes, S. (2005). *Power: A Radical View*, 2nd ed. Basingstoke: Palgrave Macmillan.

Lund-Thomsen, P. (2022). *Rethinking Global Value Chains and Corporate Social Responsibility.* Cheltenham: Edward Elgar Publishing.

Lund-Thomsen, P. & Coe, N. M. (2015). Corporate social responsibility and labour agency: The case of Nike in Pakistan. *Journal of Economic Geography*, 15(2), 275–96.

Lund-Thomsen, P. & Lindgreen, A. (2014). Corporate social responsibility in global value chains: Where are we now and where are we going? *Journal of Business Ethics*, 123, 11–22.

Lund-Thomsen, P., Lindgreen, A., & Vanhamme, J. (2016). Industrial clusters and corporate social responsibility in developing countries: What we know, what we don't, and what we need to know. *Journal of Business Ethics*, 133 (1), 9–24.

Lund-Thomsen, P., Nadvi, K., Chan, A., Khara, N., & Xue, H. (2012). Labour in global value chains: Work conditions in football manufacturing in China, India and Pakistan. *Development and Change*, 43(6), 1211–37.

Lund-Thomsen, P., Riisgaard, L., Singh, S., Ghori, S., & Coe, N. M. (2021). Global value chains and intermediaries in multi-stakeholder initiatives in Pakistan and India. *Development and Change*, 52(3), 504–32.

Lundvall, B. Å. (2016). National systems of innovation: Towards a theory of innovation and interactive learning. In B. Å. Lundvall, ed., *The Learning Economy and the Economics of Hope*. London: Anthem Press, pp. 85–106.

Maclean, R. (2022). 'Everyone's looking for plastic': As waste rises, so does recycling. *New York Times*, 31 January. www.nytimes.com/2022/01/31/world/africa/senegal-plastic-waste-recycling.html (accessed 28 April 2022).

Maresova, P., Javanmardi, E., Maskuriy, R., Selamat, A., & Kuca, K. (2022). Dynamic sustainable business modelling: Exploring the dynamics of business model components considering the product development framework. *Applied Economics*, 54(51), 5904–31.

Markard, J., Geels, F. W., & Raven, R. (2020). Challenges in the acceleration of sustainability transitions. *Environmental Research Letters*, 15(8), 081001.

Markovic, S. & Tollin, K. (2021). Business model innovation for sustainability: The intersections among business models, innovation, and sustainability. In S. Markovic, C. Sancha, & A. Lindgreen, eds., *Handbook of Sustainability-Driven Business Strategies in Practice*. Cheltenham: Edward Elgar Publishing, pp. 144–57.

Marks & Spencer. (2012). *The Key Lessons from the Plan A Business Case*. London: Marks & Spencer. https://corporate.marksandspencer.com/docu ments/plan-a-our-approach/key-lessons-from-the-plana-business-case-sep tember2012.pdf (accessed 28 April 2022).

Marques, J. C. (2019). Private regulatory capture via harmonization: An analysis of global retailer regulatory intermediaries. *Regulation & Governance*, 13(2), 157–76.

Martinuzzi, A., Krumay, B., & Pisano, U. (2011), *Focus CSR: The New Communication of the EU Commission on CSR and National CSR Strategies and Action Plans*, European Sustainable Development Network Quarterly Report No. 23. Vienna: Vienna University of Economics and Business. www.esdn.eu/fileadmin/ESDN_Reports/2011-December-The_New_Communication_of_the_EU_Commission_on_CSR_and_National_CSR_strategies.pdf (accessed 28 April 2022).

Masters, B. (2022). Supply chain bottlenecks: 'It's been nuts'. *Financial Times*, 22 January. www.ft.com/content/a3e973df-d6da-48c2-a43c-3a8acc2f1a5c (accessed 28 April 2022).

McDonald, G. (2018). The future of sustainable fashion: Mushroom leather and synthetic spider silk. *Seeker*, 24 April. www.seeker.com/tech/the-future-of-sustainable-fashion-mushroom-leather-and-synthetic-spider-silk (accessed 28 April 2022).

Microfiberinnovation (2023). Werewool fibers. [Online]. www.microfiberinnovation.org/innovation/werewool-fibers (accessed 24 January 2023).

Mieres, F. & McGrath, S. (2021). Ripe to be heard: Worker voice in the Fair Food Program. *International Labour Review*, 160(4), 631–47.

Miller, D. (2011). Global social relations and corporate social responsibility in outsourced apparel supply chains: The Inditex Global Framework Agreement. In K. Papadakis, ed., *Shaping Global Industrial Relations*. London: Palgrave Macmillan, pp. 179–98.

Montiel, I. (2008). Corporate social responsibility and corporate sustainability: Separate pasts, common futures. *Organization & Environment*, 21(3), 245–69.

Muthu, S. S. & Gardetti, M. A. (2020). *Sustainability in the Textile and Apparel Industries: Sustainable Textiles, Clothing Design and Repurposing*. Cham: Springer.

Nadvi, K. (2014). 'Rising powers' and labour and environmental standards. *Oxford Development Studies*, 42(2), 137–50.

Neilson, J. & Pritchard, B. (2009). *Value Chain Struggles: Institutions and Governance in the Plantation Districts of South India*. Chichester: Wiley-Blackwell.

Neilson, J. & Pritchard, B. (2010). Fairness and ethicality in their place: The regional dynamics of fair trade and ethical sourcing agendas in the plantation districts of South India. *Environment and Planning A*, 42(8), 1833–51.

Nelson R. R. & Winter, S. G. (1982). *An Evolutionary Theory of Economic Change*. Cambridge, MA: Belknap Press.

Nevens, F., Frantzeskaki, N., Gorissen, L., & Loorbach, D. (2013). Urban transition labs: Co-creating transformative action for sustainable cities. *Journal of Cleaner Production*, 50, 111–22.

Nill, J. & Kemp, R. (2009). Evolutionary approaches for sustainable innovation policies: From niche to paradigm? *Research Policy*, 38(4), 668–80.

OECD (Organisation for Economic Co-operation and Development). (2018). *OECD Due Diligence Guidance for Responsible Supply Chains in the Garment and Footwear Sector*. Paris: OECD Publishing.

OECD (Organisation for Economic Co-operation and Development). (2019). *Annual Report on the OECD Guidelines for Multinational Enterprises 2019*. Paris: OECD Publishing. http://mneguidelines.oecd.org/2019-Annual-Report-MNE-Guidelines-EN.pdf (accessed 28 April 2022).

OECD (Organisation for Economic Co-operation and Development). (2020). *OECD Feasibility Study: Measuring the Uptake and Impact of Due Diligence in the Garment and Footwear Sector Supply Chain*. Paris: OECD Publishing.

OECD (Organisation for Economic Co-operation and Development) & Eurostat. (2018). *Oslo Manual 2018: Guidelines for Collecting, Reporting and Using Data on Innovation*, 4th ed. Paris: OECD Publishing.

Oka, C. (2018). Brands as labour rights advocates? Potential and limits of brand advocacy in global supply chains. *Business Ethics: A European Review*, 27 (2), 95–107.

Oka, C., Egels-Zandén, N., & Alexander, R. (2020). Buyer engagement and labour conditions in global supply chains: The Bangladesh accord and beyond. *Development and Change*, 51(5), 1306–30.

Oka, C., Egels-Zandén, N., Rahman, S., & Alexander, R. (2020). *Scale Matters: Scalability of Business Case Sustainability Initiatives in the Garment Industry*. Egham: Royal Holloway University of London.

Oliver, C. (1991). Strategic responses to institutional processes. *Academy of Management Review*, 16, 145–179.

O'Rourke, D. & Ringer, A. (2016). The impact of sustainability information on consumer decision making. *Journal of Industrial Ecology*, 20(4), 882–92.

Palacios-Mateo, C., van der Meer, Y., & Seide, G. (2021). Analysis of the polyester clothing value chain to identify key intervention points for sustainability. *Environmental Sciences Europe*, 33(2), 1–25.

Palpacuer, F. & Smith, A. (2021). *Rethinking Value Chains: Tackling the Challenges of Global Capitalism*. Bristol: Policy Press.

Pasquali, G., Godfrey, S., & Nadvi, K. (2021). Understanding regional value chains through the interaction of public and private governance: Insights from Southern Africa's apparel sector. *Journal of International Business Policy*, 4(3), 368–89.

Peters, G., Li, M., & Lenzen, M. (2021). The need to decelerate fast fashion in a hot climate: A global sustainability perspective on the garment industry on the garment industry. *Journal of Cleaner Production*, 295, 126390.

Pietrobelli, C. & Rabellotti, R. (2011). Global value chains meet innovation systems: Are there learning opportunities for developing countries? *World Development*, 39(7), 1261–9.

Pietrobelli, C. & Staritz, C. (2018). Upgrading, interactive learning, and innovation systems in value chain interventions. *The European Journal of Development Research*, 30, 557–74.

Ponte, S. (2019). *Business, Power and Sustainability in a World of Global Value Chains*. London: Bloomsbury Publishing.

Ponte, S. (2020). Green capital accumulation: Business and sustainability management in a world of global value chains. *New Political Economy*, 25 (1), 72–84.

Ponte, S., Gereffi, G., & Raj-Reichert, G. (2019). Introduction to the handbook on global value chains. In S. Ponte, G. Gereffi, & G. Raj-Reichert, eds., *Handbook on Global Value Chains*. Cheltenham: Edward Elgar Publishing, pp. 1–28.

Ponte, S. & Gibbon, P. (2005). Quality standards, conventions and the governance of global value chains. *Economy and Society*, 34(1), 1–31.

Ponte, S. & Sturgeon, T. (2014). Explaining governance in global value chains: A modular theory-building effort. *Review of International Political Economy*, 21(1), 195–223.

Raj-Reichert, G. (2019). The role of transnational first-tier suppliers in GVC governance. In S. Ponte, G. Gereffi, & G. Raj-Reichert, eds., *Handbook on Global Value Chains*. Cheltenham: Edward Elgar Publishing, pp. 354–69.

Rana, M. B. & Allen, M. C. (2021). *Upgrading the Global Garment Industry: Internationalization, Capabilities and Sustainability*. Cheltenham: Edward Elgar Publishing.

Reinales, D., Zambrana Vásquez, D., & Sáez de Guinoa, A. (2020). Social life cycle assessment of product value chains under a circular economy approach: A case study in the plastic packaging sector. *Sustainability*, 12(16), 1–17.

Remington, C. (2022). Microfiber innovation challenge winners named. *Ecotextile News*, 18 March. www.ecotextile.com/2022031829095/materials-production-news/microfiber-innovation-challenge-winners-named.html (accessed 28 April 2022).

Riddselius, C. (2010). *Fashion Victims: A Report on Sandblasted Denim*. Stockholm: Fair Trade Center.

Riisgaard, L., Lund-Thomsen, P., & Coe, N. M. (2020). Multistakeholder initiatives in global production networks: Naturalizing specific understandings of sustainability through the Better Cotton Initiative. *Global Networks*, 20(2), 211–36.

Roberts-Islam, B. (2021). The new automated jeans factory in L.A.: A blueprint for reshoring apparel manufacturing? *Forbes*, 10 March. www.forbes.com/sites/brookerobertsislam/2021/03/10/the-new-auto mated-jeans-factory-in-la-a-blueprint-for-reshoring-apparel-manufactur ing (accessed 28 April 2022).

Rotmans, J., Kemp, R., & Van Asselt, M. (2001). More evolution than revolution: Transition management in public policy, *Foresight*, 3(1), 15–31.

Rushe, D., Connolly, K., Giuffrida, A., Hannam, P., & Ellis-Petersen, H. (2022). The rise in global inflation: The hit to living standards across the world. *The Guardian*, 10 February. www.theguardian.com/business/2022/feb/10/the-rise-in-global-inflation-the-hit-to-living-standards-across-the-world (accessed 28 April 2022).

Ruwanpura, K. N., & Wrigley, N. (2011). The costs of compliance? Views of Sri Lankan apparel manufacturers in times of global economic crisis. *Journal of Economic Geography*, 11(6), 1031–1049.

Ruwanpura, K. (2022). Doing the right thing? COVID-19, PPE and the case of Sri Lankan apparels. *Global Labor Journal*, 13(1), 110–21.

Šajn, N. (2019). *Environmental Impact of the Textile and Clothing Industry: What Consumers Need to Know*. Brussels: European Parliamentary Research Service.

Schaltegger, S. & Wagner, M. (2011). Sustainable entrepreneurship and sustainability innovation: Categories and interactions. *Business Strategy and the Environment*, 20(4), 222–37.

Schmitz, H. (2006). Learning and earning in global garment and footwear chains. *The European Journal of Development Research*, 18(4), 546–71.

Schüßler, E., Frenkel, S. J., Ashwin, S. et al. (2018). *Changes in the Governance of Garment Global Production Networks: Lead Firm, Supplier and Institutional Responses to the Rana Plaza Disaster, Garment Supply Chain Governance*. Interim Report, November. Berlin: Garment Supply Chain Governance Project.

Schwab, K. (2016). *The Fourth Industrial Revolution*. Geneva: World Economic Forum.

Schwab, K. & Davis, N. (2018). *Shaping the Future of the Fourth Industrial Revolution: A Guide to Building a Better World*. Geneva: World Economic Forum.

Scott, W. R. (2013). *Institutions and Organizations: Ideas, Interests, and Identities*. Thousand Oaks, CA: Sage Publications.

Searcy, C., Kapuscinski, A. R., & Dooley, K. (2017). Multi-stakeholder initiatives in sustainable supply chains: Putting sustainability performance in context. *Elementa: Science of the Anthropocene*, 5, 73. doi.org/10.1525/elementa.262.

Serdijn, M., Kolk, A., & Fransen, L. (2020). Uncovering missing links in global value chain research – and implications for corporate social responsibility and international business. *Critical Perspectives on International Business*, 17(4), 619–36.

Silvestre, B. S., Silva, M. E., Cormack, A., & Thome, A. M. T. (2020). Supply chain sustainability trajectories: Learning through sustainability initiatives. *International Journal of Operations and Production Management*, 40(9), 1301–37.

Simchi-Levi, S. & Haren, P. (2022). How the war in Ukraine is further disrupting global supply chains. *Harvard Business Review*, 17 March. https://hbr.org/2022/03/how-the-war-in-ukraine-is-further-disrupting-global-supply-chains (accessed 28 April 2022).

Siroën, J. M. (2013). Labour provisions in preferential trade agreements: Current practice and outlook. *International Labour Review*, 152(1), 85–106.

Smit, L., Bright, C., McCorquodale, R. et al. (2020). *Study on Due Diligence Requirements through the Supply Chain: Final Report*. Brussels: European Commission.

Smith, A., Stirling, A., & Berkhout, F. (2005). The governance of sustainable socio-technical transitions. *Research Policy*, 34(10), 1491–1510.

Soundararajan, V. & Brammer, S. (2018). Developing country sub-supplier responses to social sustainability requirements of intermediaries: Exploring the influence of framing on fairness perceptions and reciprocity. *Journal of Operations Management*, 58, 42–58.

Soundararajan, V., Brown, J. A., & Wicks, A. C. (2019). Can multi-stakeholder initiatives improve global supply chains? Improving deliberative capacity with a stakeholder orientation. *Business Ethics Quarterly*, 29(3), 385–412.

Soundararajan, V., Khan, Z., & Tarba, S. Y. (2018). Beyond brokering: Sourcing agents, boundary work and working conditions in global supply chains. *Human Relations*, 71(4), 481–509.

Stankevich, A. (2017). Explaining the consumer decision-making process: Critical literature review. *Journal of International Business Research and Marketing*, 2(6), 7–14.

Statista. (2022). *Revenue of Fashion Retail Companies in India FY 2022*. New York: Statista. www.statista.com/statistics/1327326/india-fashion-retail-companies-revenue (accessed 23 January 2023).

Steubing, B., Mutel, C., Suter, F., & Hellweg, S. (2016). Streamlining scenario analysis and optimization of key choices in value chains using a modular LCA approach. *The International Journal of Life Cycle Assessment*, 21, 510–22.

Steurer, R., Margula, S., & Martinuzzi, A. (2012). Public policies on CSR in Europe: Themes, instruments, and regional differences. University of Natural Resources and Life Sciences Discussion Paper 2-2012.

Strambach, S. (2017). Combining knowledge bases in transnational sustainability innovation: Microdynamics and institutional change. *Economic Geography*, 93(5), 500–26.

Strambach, S. & Surmeier, A. (2018). From standard takers to standard makers? The role of knowledge-intensive intermediaries in setting global sustainability standards. *Global Networks*, 18(2), 352–73.

Sturgeon, T. (2019). Measuring global value chains. In S. Ponte, G. Gereffi, & G. Raj-Reichert, eds., *Handbook on Global Value Chains*. Cheltenham: Edward Elgar Publishing, pp. 77–90.

Surmeier, A. (2020). Dynamic capability building and social upgrading in tourism: Potentials and limits of sustainability standards. *Journal of Sustainable Tourism*, 28(10), 1498–1518.

Sustainable Brands. (2016). PUMA launches financing program to reward suppliers for sustainability performance. [Online]. https://sustainablebrands.com/ read/organizational-change/puma-launches-financing-program-to-reward-sup pliers-for-sustainability-performance (accessed 28 April 2022).

Sutradhar, A., Bhuiyan, M. H. R., Mazumder, F. T. et al. (2021). Devising a dust and noise pollution monitoring system for textile industry. In Bangladesh University of Engineering and Technology, ed., *Proceedings of the 8th International Conference on Networking, Systems and Security*. New York: Association for Computing Machinery, pp. 77–82.

Teece, D. J. (2010). Technological innovation and the theory of the firm: The role of enterprise-level knowledge, complementarities and (dynamic) capabilities, In B. H. Hall & N. Rosenberg, eds., *Handbook of the Economics of Innovation*. Amsterdam: North-Holland, pp. 679–730.

Tewari, M. (2017). Relational contracting at the bottom of global garment value chains: Lessons from Mewat. *The Indian Journal of Labour Economics*, 60 (2), 137–54.

Tiernan, J. (2019). PrimaLoft Bio insulation. [Online]. https://outdoorsmagic .com/article/primaloft-bio-insulation-gear-news (accessed 28 April 2022).

Tokatli, N. & Kizilgün, Ö. (2009). From manufacturing garments for ready-to-wear to designing collections for fast-fashion: Evidence from Turkey, *Environment and Planning A*, 41(1), 146–62.

Tura, N., Keränen, J., & Patala, S. (2019). The darker side of sustainability: Tensions from sustainable business practices in business networks. *Industrial Marketing Management*, 77, 221–31.

UN Comtrade. (2023). UN Comtrade [database]. New York: UN Statistics Division.

UNIDO (United Nations Industrial Development Organization). (2020). *Chemical Leasing: Function to Impact*. Vienna: UNIDO.

United Nations (2015). *Transforming Our World: The 2030 Agenda for Sustainable Development*. A/RES/70/1. New York: United Nations Department of Economic and Social Affairs.

United Nations (n.d.). The Paris Agreement. [Online]. www.un.org/en/climate change/paris-agreement# (accessed 26 January 2023).

Van der Ven, H. & Cashore, B. (2018). Forest certification: The challenge of measuring impacts. *Current Opinion in Environmental Sustainability*, 32, 104–11.

Van Mierlo, B. & Beers, P. J. (2020). Understanding and governing learning in sustainability transitions: A review. *Environmental Innovation and Societal Transitions*, 34, 255–69.

Vitols, K. & Voss, E. (2019). *Social Conditions in Logistics in Europe: Focus on Road Transport. Final Report*. Berlin: EVA (Europäische Akademie für umweltorientierten Verkehr gGmbH). https://psl.verdi.de/++file++5d00b20c9194fb 1d8bbc127f/download/Social%20Conditions%20Logistics%20in%20Europe .pdf (accessed 28 April 2022).

von Broembsen, M. (2020). Regulating corporations in global value chains to realise labour rights for homeworkers. In M. Chen & F. Carré, eds., *The Informal Economy Revisited*. Abingdon: Routledge, pp. 143–50.

World Commission on Economic Development. (1987). *Our Common Future*. Oxford: Oxford University Press.

Yoon, S. & Nadvi, K. (2018). Industrial clusters and industrial ecology: Building 'eco-collective efficiency' in a South Korean cluster. *Geoforum*, 90, 159–73.

Zahra, S. A. & George, G. (2002). Absorptive capacity: A review, reconceptualization, and extension. *Academy of Management Review*, 27(2), 185–203.

Zero Discharge of Hazardous Chemicals Programme. (2016). *Textile Industry Wastewater Discharge Quality Standards: Literature Review*. Amsterdam: ZDHC Foundation.

Zhang, T. (2022). Here are the 10 biggest Chinese apparel companies. *Women's Wear Daily*, 5 July.

Acknowledgements

The authors would like to acknowledge the support of the Ministry of Foreign Affairs of Denmark and the Danida Fellowship Center for funding part of the work undertaken to write this Element under the research and research capacity development grant 'Climate Change and Global Value Chains in Bangladesh' (Grant No. 20–10-CBS). The research undertaken for writing this Element is independent and the views and opinions expressed are solely those of the authors. They should not be attributed to the Ministry of Foreign Affairs of Denmark.

We would also like to express gratitude to J.-C. Spender for his support through the editing process. Additionally, we would like to thank Naveen Prasath, Felinda Sharmal, and Linsey Hague for their help in getting the final Element together. Finally, we would like to thank the two anonymous reviewers for their comments and suggestions on an earlier draft. All errors or omissions are the authors' own.

Business Strategy

J.-C. Spender
Kozminski University

J.-C. Spender is a research Professor, Kozminski University. He has been active in the business strategy field since 1971 and is the author or co-author of 7 books and numerous papers. His principal academic interest is in knowledge-based theories of the private sector firm, and managing them.

About the Series

Business strategy's reach is vast, and important too since wherever there is business activity there is strategizing. As a field, strategy has a long history from medieval and colonial times to today's developed and developing economies. This series offers a place for interesting and illuminating research including industry and corporate studies, strategizing in service industries, the arts, the public sector, and the new forms of Internet-based commerce. It also covers today's expanding gamut of analytic techniques.

Cambridge Elements ☰

Business Strategy

Printed in the United States
by Baker & Taylor Publisher Services